More Advance Praise for *Leading with Cultural Intelligence:*

"Successful global leadership requires IQ, EQ—emotional intelligence, and, increasingly, CQ. In this practical, highly readable, evidence-based book on Cultural Intelligence David Livermore helps us complete this vital triad of capabilities."

> —**Richard O. Mason, Carr P. Collins Distinguished Professor, Emeritus,**
> **Southern Methodist University, Dallas Texas**

"Everywhere is now part of everywhere else. *Leading with Cultural Intelligence* is an essential guide to navigating that new reality."

> —**Gregg Easterbrook, author,** *Sonic Boom* **and** *Progress Paradox*

"David Livermore offers real-life observations and insights that will enhance your ability to navigate cultural diversity in a global environment that is constantly changing. This book will definitely enhance your ability to lead and serve others. I know it helped raise my cultural intelligence."

> —**Mike Volkema, Chairman, Herman Miller, Inc.**

"If *Cultural Intelligence* (CQ) is currently the most important theory and measure of cross-cultural competence in the field, then *Leading with Cultural Intelligence* by David Livermore is the foremost manual for practicing CQ there is. As a multicultural educator, I admire David's ability to succinctly translate sophisticated science into very practical prose. As a trainer of psychologists, counselors, and other mental health professionals, I am struck by how simple, applicable, and effective David's model is for students and practitioners in my field who strive for cultural competence. And, finally, as a lifelong cultural aficionado, I find the many examples and stories to be at once poignant and inspiring."

> —**Michael Goh, Ph.D., Director of Counseling Program,**
> **University of Minnesota**

"Coupling personal experience with definitive cross-cultural theory, David Livermore's *Leading with Cultural Intelligence* is a painless tutorial that prompts readers to individualize Ang and Earley's notion of 'CQ.' Whether by 'strolling through a grocery store,' applying a 'why, why, why, strategy,' distinguishing 'event time from clock time,' or considering 'a culture's artistic system,' this primer is brimming with practical ideas for invigorating one's quest to lead more intelligently in a global world."

> —**Priscilla Rogers, Ph.D., Associate Professor of Business Communication,**
> **Ross School of Business, University of Michigan**

"As more companies go global, we need a better understanding of how to function as leaders across cultural boundaries. Enter David Livermore's new book, *Leading with Cultural Intelligence.* Read how David's four-step process can help you develop your 'CQ' and improve your cross-cultural leadership technique. Now more than ever, our shrinking world needs what's in this book!"

> —**Ken Blanchard, coauthor of** *The One Minute Manager*® **and**
> *Leading at a Higher Level*

"For those leaders who want to succeed in today's increasingly global and inter-dependent environment, David Livermore's *Leading with Cultural Intelligence* is for you. Now, more than ever, applying this simple four-step cycle will prepare you for tomorrow's world."

—**Paul Polman, Chief Executive Officer, Unilever**

"For a very long time now we've mostly been acting like tourists on holiday when traveling through the global economy. We stay just long enough to taste the cuisine, see the sights, and enjoy the ambience . . . but we never really adapt ourselves to a new culture. As the world continues to flatten, and as our economies become increasingly global, this kind of tourist leadership is unsustainable. A fundamental transformation must take place in how we lead diverse groups of people who are culturally different from the leader, and often culturally different from each other. Thankfully, with David Livermore's new book, *Leading with Cultural Intelligence*, we finally have a resource that can help us navigate this relatively new territory. In this inspired and intensely enjoyable work, Livermore brilliantly presents a fresh new way of grappling with the nuances and complexities of cross-cultural experiences. Based on solid academic research and years of personal experience, *Leading with Cultural Intelligence* offers a whole new way of thinking holistically about the challenges and presents a repertoire of skills and behaviors that we can put to use in cross-cultural interactions. Livermore's exceptionally vivid examples of cultural dilemmas bring the book to life, and his descriptions of ways to apply the principles of cultural intelligence to our own leadership struggles make it a highly practical guide. *Leading with Cultural Intelligence* is a groundbreaking book that is a must-read for every twenty-first-century leader."

—**Jim Kouzes, award-winning coauthor of the best-selling book**
***The Leadership Challenge* and Dean's Executive Professor of Leadership,**
Leavey School of Business, Santa Clara University

"David Livermore has written a must-read book for anyone who interacts with people from different cultures. He embeds his suggestions for working cross-culturally in a framework that is based on sound theory and empirical evidence about Cultural Intelligence while also including engaging stories and very doable activities. I will adopt this book whenever I teach MBAs, managers, or executives about culture."

—**Lynn Shore, Professor of Management and Co-Director,**
Institute for Inclusiveness and Diversity in Organizations,
San Diego State University

"Dave Livermore's *Leading with Cultural Intelligence* is an essential tool for working, living and leading in a world without borders."

—**Dick DeVos, President, The Windquest Group,**
and former president of Amway Global

"This book should be required reading for every business school student, both the undergraduate and graduate students, and *especially* those Ph.D. students! The next generation of leaders needs to start working now on their CQ. I am grateful to David Livermore for putting this knowledge into such a readable and informative package."

—**Cynthia Beath, Professor Emerita, McCombs School of Business,**
University of Texas at Austin

Leading with Cultural Intelligence

The New Secret to Success

David Livermore, Ph.D.

Foreword by Soon Ang, Ph.D., and Linn Van Dyne, Ph.D.

AMACOM

American Management Association

New York • Atlanta • Brussels • Chicago • Mexico City • San Francisco
Shanghai • Tokyo • Toronto • Washington, D.C.

Special discounts on bulk quantities of AMACOM books are available to corporations, professional associations, and other organizations. For details, contact Special Sales Department, AMACOM, a division of American Management Association, 1601 Broadway, New York, NY 10019.
Tel: 800-250-5308. Fax: 518-891-2372.
E-mail: specialsls@amanet.org
Website: www.amacombooks.org/go/specialsales
To view all AMACOM titles go to: www.amacombooks.org

This publication is designed to provide accurate and authoritative information in regard to the subject matter covered. It is sold with the understanding that the publisher is not engaged in rendering legal, accounting, or other professional service. If legal advice or other expert assistance is required, the services of a competent professional person should be sought.

Library of Congress Cataloging-in-Publication Data

Livermore, David A., 1967–
  Leading with cultural intelligence : the new secret to success / David Livermore ; foreword by Soon Ang and Linn Van Dyne.
    p. cm.
  Includes index.
  ISBN-13: 978-0-8144-1487-3 (hardcover)
  ISBN-10: 0-8144-1487-7 (hardcover)
  1. Leadership—Cross-cultural studies. 2. Organizational behavior—Cross-cultural studies. 3. Management—Cross-cultural studies. 4. Intercultural communication. 5. Cross-cultural orientation. I. Title.
  HD57.7.L589 2010
  658.4'092—dc22
                              2009015446

Printing number

10 9 8 7 6 5 4 3

For Linda . . . my ultimate soul mate,
fellow sojourner, and love

CONTENTS

We are pleased to write the foreword to David Livermore's latest book on cultural intelligence (CQ). We have known Dave professionally for many years and have followed his work with great interest. Dave has always had a passion for intercultural training and education and has spent several years training leaders to serve on short-term overseas assignments.

As academic professors who pioneered the research and basic science of cultural intelligence in organizational behavior and cross-cultural psychology, we were introduced to Dave by a mutual colleague. The colleague thought our academic research on cultural intelligence could influence Dave's work in the field *and* Dave's vast intercultural experiences could help us refine our own thinking about cultural intelligence.

Few people can translate technical academic work into clear and lucid material. Dave has done just that with this book on culturally intelligent leadership. Dave is especially qualified to write this book. He has a Ph.D. in the field of education, with special emphasis on multicultural education. He understands the importance of evidence-based management principles and emphasizes research-based scientific evidence rather than anecdotes as the basis for his key points. As a result, *Leading with Cultural Intelligence* presents a view of leadership that is solidly grounded on cultural intelligence theory and research. By drawing on key concepts and ideas that have been well validated academically, Dave accurately brings alive the concept of cultural intelligence and applies it with highly practical how-to's for global businesses and practitioners.

The book is easy to read and highly relevant for today's managers and global leaders who must grapple with the complexities of cultural differences. Dave uses rich and vivid real-life examples throughout all chapters in the book.

Dave begins the book by explaining the importance of cultural intelligence in today's organizations and illustrating why cultural intelligence is critical for leadership effectiveness. He then systematically describes the four-step CQ cycle that includes regulating your own motivation to learn about other cultures, acquiring knowledge of other cultures, becoming more aware of yourself and others who are culturally different, and adapting your behavior to fit other cultures.

Dave describes each step in the cycle clearly and succinctly, and he ends each chapter in Part II with a series of highly practical action steps. These suggestions serve as starting points for those who wish to develop their own CQ so as to leverage their diverse cultural experiences effectively.

This book is for those in all kinds of leadership positions. It is also especially relevant to global leaders, multicultural teams, human resource managers, management training and development professionals, organizational researchers, and students. It should interest anyone who wants to better understand the factors that are critical to effective leadership in our multicultural, global world.

It is indeed a rare privilege to be asked to write a foreword to a book that will become the quintessential guidebook for global leadership in the twenty-first century and beyond.

—Soon Ang, Ph.D.
Goh Tjoei Kok Chair and Professor in Management
Center for Leadership & Cultural Intelligence
Nanyang Business School
Nanyang Technological University, Singapore

—Linn Van Dyne, Ph.D.
Professor in Management
Michigan State University
East Lansing, Michigan

We've all seen it. Some leaders move in and out of various cultural contexts as effortlessly as an Olympic ice skater performing a gold-medal routine. And others look more like me when I stumble around our local ice rink on a once-a-year outing with my kids. What makes the difference? Why are some leaders more effective managing across cultural borders than others? Why is it some leaders effectively create trust and negotiate contracts with Latin Americans, Chinese, and Germans all in the same day while others stumble to manage the diversity in their own offices? Most important, what is the difference between leaders who demonstrate genuine respect for people who see the world differently and those who don't? That's what this book is about—learning to lead with cultural intelligence. *Cultural intelligence*, or CQ, is your "capability to function effectively across national, ethnic, and organizational cultures."[1] Rather than expecting you to master all of the norms of the various cultures encountered, cultural intelligence helps you develop an overall repertoire and perspective that results in more effective leadership. Cultural intelligence is both a capability and an overall model for thinking about cross-cultural leadership. Throughout the book, the terms *intercultural* and *cross-cultural* are used synonymously. Although technically the terms differ (*cross-cultural* referring to "two cultures interacting" and *intercultural* referring to "several cultures interacting"), I've followed the norm of many authors in using the two terms interchangeably, with the primary use of the familiar term *cross-cultural.*

Why This Book?

The purpose of this book is to show you how to lead with cultural intelligence. Rooted in research across twenty-five countries, this book gives you a four-step cycle that can be applied to any cross-cultural situation. Nobody ever leads across cultures perfectly, but by learning and applying these four steps, you can improve the way you lead and relate across numerous national, ethnic, and organizational cultures.

There's an abundance of books and models available on global management and cross-cultural leadership. Many of these sources have informed my own thinking and practice. However, 70 percent of international ventures continue to fail because of cultural differences.[2] Simplistic approaches that teach cultural practices and taboos aren't sufficient. However, some books on culture and leadership are so complex and cerebral that it's tempting to toss them aside as little more than ivory-tower rhetoric.

Leading with Cultural Intelligence is unique from other cross-cultural leadership titles in that it provides a coherent, research-based framework (cultural intelligence) for success in a diversity of cultural contexts. It's written for professionals working in a wide range of settings, including business, government, and nonprofit. The four-step cycle (CQ drive, CQ knowledge, CQ strategy, and CQ action) presented in this book can be applied to any multicultural situation.

Research Basis

The cultural intelligence model is rooted in rigorous empirical work, which spans researchers from twenty-five countries. Researchers Christopher Earley and Soon Ang built on the research on multiple intelligences to develop the conceptual model of cultural intelligence.[3] As a twenty-item inventory, the Cultural Intelligence Scale was developed and validated to measure CQ across multiple cultures.[4] CQ predicts many important aspects of cross-cultural effectiveness and provides a solid basis for scientific work. Since 2003, CQ has attracted worldwide attention across diverse disciplines. Although it has been tested most thoroughly in business and educational contexts, data has also been collected from the fields of nursing, engineering, law, consulting, mental health, government, and religion.[5]

The research referenced throughout the book comes from a number of the researchers engaged in testing cultural intelligence, including myself. Any of the data drawn directly from the research of others is cited as such. In particular, Dr. Soon Ang at Nanyang Technological University in Singapore and Dr. Linn Van Dyne at Michigan State University have generously shared their research, insights, and time from several years of researching cultural intelligence. The three of us are working closely together in researching and applying cultural intelligence and you'll note references to their work throughout the book. My own research on cultural intelligence has been qualitative in nature, although always informed by the quantitative work of others. A brief description of the nature and methodology of my research is found in the appendix. To respect and protect the confidentiality of those surveyed, the names of subjects and their organizations have been changed; however, other demographic information (e.g., gender, age, ethnicity, and basic location) have not been altered in the reporting of the findings throughout the book.

How to Read This Book

Think of *Leading with Cultural Intelligence* as a field guide for understanding and developing cultural intelligence in yourself and others. CQ isn't a destination per se but an ability that serves as a compass for guiding us through the globalized world of leadership. Nobody gets to the end of this journey. But with some effort, we'll perform better.

Some leaders have little time to read much more than a quick summary of ideas. If you're that kind of reader, you can jump through the book and gain the gist of the four-step model by reading the shaded summaries that run throughout the book. Others will want the fuller picture that comes with stories and explanation. That's here too. I encourage you to read this book in whatever way suits you best.

Chapter 1 explains the relevance of cultural intelligence to leadership. Although most leaders readily acknowledge the multicultural landscape of today's leadership journey, we'll examine some recurring reasons why a capability like cultural intelligence is uniquely suited to the twenty-first-century leadership challenge. Chapter 2 provides an overview of the cultural intelligence model, including a brief description of the four dimensions of cultural intelligence. Chapters 3 to 7 present the most important section of the book—the four steps for becoming more culturally intelligent. These four steps are a cycle we can run through before taking on any cross-cultural assignment. The final two chapters, Chapters 8 and 9, review the key ways to develop CQ in yourself and your organization.

This book has been deeply personal for me to write because I do not write as one merely standing on the outside, observing the cross-cultural leadership of others. I've spent the last couple decades in leadership roles with people from a vast array of cultural backgrounds across several different countries. I have as many failures as successes in my own attempts to lead cross-culturally. And I've spent the last several years researching the phenomenon of cross-cultural leadership in others. So the book includes research data exemplified through real-life stories to offer some best practices for cross-cultural leadership.

What an exciting time! It's virtually free to talk with someone on the other side of the world. The causes dear to our hearts can touch the lives of people living fifteen time zones away. We get to learn from leaders working and managing in vastly different places from us. We can eat nachos in Bangkok, sushi in Johannesburg, and baklava in Omaha. We can tap the accounting skills of professionals in Bangalore. And despite rising fuel costs, the opportunity to see the world firsthand and interact with people from around the planet has never been more possible. With cultural intelligence, we can engage in our rapidly shrinking world with an underlying sense of mutual respect and dignity for people everywhere. This book provides a pathway for gracefully and successfully embarking on the journey into a shrinking world. I'm grateful to share the journey with you.

—David Livermore
Grand Rapids, Michigan

ACKNOWLEDGMENTS

My professional colleague and friend, Steve Argue, shares every project with me. Whether it's talking me off the ledge, pushing me to improve what's there, or offering his very creative mind, I can't write without his input.

This is a different book because of Soon Ang, Dick DeVos, Rebecca Kuiper, Linda Fenty, Don Maine, Kok Yee Ng, Sandra Upton, Linn Van Dyne, and Mike Volkema. Each of them read a really rough draft of the manuscript and their input profoundly shaped the end product.

There's good reason why you see the names Soon Ang and Linn Van Dyne throughout the book. They inspired me to write the book and made it possible by so generously sharing their research, insights, critiques, and encouragement. I'm grateful to be partnering with them on how to take the research and application of cultural intelligence further.

Christina Parisi, my editor at AMACOM, first responded to my proposal by saying, "Ever since I went abroad in college, I've had an interest in this topic." Her personal resonance with the topic silenced other publishers' bids. And the partnership throughout the development of the book has been deeply gratifying.

My oldest daughter, Emily, is growing up to be a culturally intelligent young woman who engages in great dialogues with me. And my daughter Grace's love for life and her ability to "say it like it is" make me laugh and keep life in perspective for me. My wife, Linda, shared in each iteration of this project, from its mere infancy as an idea to the final touches. Her love, debate, encouragement, and partnership are a gift to me like none other.

Part I

What Is CQ and Why Do I Need It?

CHAPTER 1

YOU LEAD ACROSS A MULTICULTURAL TERRAIN:
WHY CQ?

Leadership today is a multicultural challenge. Few of us need to be convinced of that fact. We're competing in a global marketplace, managing a diverse workforce, and trying to keep up with rapidly shifting trends. However, many approaches to this leadership challenge seem either far too simplistic (e.g., "Smile, avoid these three taboos, and you'll be fine") or far too extreme (e.g., "Don't go anywhere until you're a cross-cultural guru"). Cultural intelligence offers a better way. The four-step cycle of cultural intelligence presented in this book is one you can run through every time you jump into a new cross-cultural situation.

What are the biggest hindrances to reaching your goals personally and professionally? How do you effectively lead people who come from different cultural backgrounds? What kinds of cultural situations bring you the greatest level of fatigue? How do you give instructions for an assignment to a Pakistani employee versus one from Bosnia? What kind of training should you design for a management team coming from multiple cultural backgrounds? How do you get feedback from a colleague who comes from a culture that values saving face above direct, straightforward feedback? And how can you possibly keep up with all the different cultural scenarios that surface in our rapidly globalizing world? These are the kinds of questions answered by running through the four-step cycle of CQ presented in this book.

All my life I've been fascinated by cultures. From as far back in my childhood as a Canadian-American kid growing up in New York, I was intrigued by the differences we'd encounter on our trips across the border to visit our relatives in Canada. The multicolored money, the different ways of saying things, and the varied cuisine we found after passing through customs drew me in. I've learned far more about leadership, global issues, and my faith from cross-cultural experiences and work than from any graduate course I've ever taken or taught. I've made people laugh when I've stumbled through a different language or inadvertently ate something the "wrong" way. I've winced upon later discovering I offended a group of ethnically different colleagues because I spent *too* much time complimenting them. I'm a better leader, teacher, father, friend, and citizen because of the cross-cultural friendships I've forged through my work. And through the fascinating domain of cultural intelligence, I've discovered an enriched way to understand and prepare for my cross-cultural work.

Cultural intelligence is the "capability to function effectively across national, ethnic, and organizational cultures."[1] It can be learned by almost anyone. Cultural intelligence offers leaders an overall repertoire and perspective that can be applied to a myriad of cultural situations. It is a capability that includes four different dimensions enabling us to meet the fast-paced demands of leadership. This book describes how to gain the competitive edge and finesse that comes from running through the four-step cycle of cultural intelligence. Think about a cross-cultural assignment or situation facing you. Take a minute and walk through the four-step cycle of CQ right now:

1. CQ Drive: What is your motivation for this assignment?

2. CQ Knowledge: What cultural information is needed to fulfill this task?

3. CQ Strategy: What is your plan for this initiative?

4. CQ Action: What behaviors do you need to adapt to do this effectively?

If you don't have a clue how to answer one or more of those questions right now, the book will explain how to do all that. But before more fully describing what cultural intelligence is and how to develop it, it is important to see its direct relevance to leadership in a rapidly globalizing world. This chapter reviews some of the most compelling reasons for becoming more culturally intelligent. We begin with a story and then we look at an overview of the relevance of cultural intelligence to our most pressing leadership demands.

From West Michigan to West Africa

It's the day before I fly to Monrovia, the capital city of Liberia. Liberia, a small country on the coast of West Africa, isn't a place I ever planned to visit. But given that my organization has recently formed a partnership there, it's now become a regular destination for me. I've spent far more time working in Europe, Asia, and Latin America, which are much more familiar destinations to me. West Africa still feels very foreign. Yet, the flattened world of globalization makes even the most foreign places still seem oddly familiar in some strange way. Wireless access in the hotel where I stay, Diet Coke, and the use of U.S. currency remove some of the faraway feeling of a place like Monrovia yet I still have to make a lot of adaptations to do my job in a place like Liberia.

It's amazing how life and work in our rapidly globalizing world brings us an unprecedented number of encounters with people, places, and issues from around the world. I guess the world is flat—isn't it? Economist Thomas Friedman popularized the term *flat world* to suggest that the competitive playing fields between industrialized and emerging markets are leveling.[2]

The day before I leave for West Africa is spent tying up loose ends prior to my weeklong absence. I respond to e-mails from colleagues in Dubai, Shanghai, Frankfurt, and Johannesburg and I talk on the phone with clients in Kuala Lumpur and Hong Kong. My wife and I grab a quick lunch at our favorite Indian restaurant, and we talk with a Sudanese refugee who bags the groceries we pick up on the way home. Before my kids return from their Cinco de Mayo celebration at school, I call my credit card company and I reach a customer service representative in Delhi. Even in the small city of Grand Rapids, Michigan, where I live, cross-cultural encounters abound.

One would think travel across the flattened world would be easier than it is. Getting from Grand Rapids to Monrovia takes some very deliberate planning and it wreaks havoc on the body. My travel and work have to be planned around the three days a week when Brussels Air, the only Western airline that flies into Monrovia, goes there. But still, the fact that I can have breakfast with my family one morning and go for a run along the Atlantic Coast in West Africa less than twenty-four hours later is still pretty amazing. So maybe the world is becoming flat.

On the flight from Brussels to Monrovia, I sit next to Tim, a twenty-two-year-old Liberian guy currently living in Atlanta. We chat briefly. He describes his enthusiasm about going home to Liberia for his first visit since his parents helped plan his escape to the United States during the civil war ten years previously.

As we land, I see the U.N. planes parked across the tarmac. A mere eight hours ago, I was walking the streets of Brussels and grabbing an early morning waffle. And here I am making my way toward passport control in Monrovia. Maybe travel across multiple time zones isn't so bad after all.

Eventually I end up at the baggage claim next to Tim, my new acquaintance. A porter who looks so old he could pass for age 100 is there to help Tim with his luggage. The porter asks Tim, "How long are you staying here, man?" Tim responds, "Only two weeks. I wish it was longer." The porter bursts out with a piercing laugh. "Why, my man? You're from the USA!" Tim responds, "I know, but life is hard there. I wish I could stay here longer. Life is better here." The porter laughs even harder, slaps Tim on the back, and says, "You're talking crazy, man. Look at you. You have an American passport!

You don't know what a hard life is. I've been working the last thirty-seven hours straight and they haven't paid me for six weeks. But I can't give up this job. Most people don't have jobs. But look at you. You've been eating well. You look so fat and healthy. And you live in the USA!" Tim just shakes his head and says, "You don't know. You have no idea, no idea. It's hard. Never mind. Just get my bag." I can see the fatigue penetrating Tim's broad shoulders.

I can understand why the porter found it absolutely laughable that a twenty-two-year-old bloke who can afford a two-week vacation across the ocean could consider life "hard." Yet I imagine there are some significant hardships for Tim as a young African-American man liv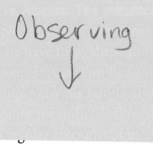re stacked against him. How many 𝕡 *Observing* ↓ hen he walks by? What extra hoops ;et hired at the fitness center where me the enormous expectations place riends who stayed back in Liberia. A pe the war, so the least he can do is s y to support them. Observing these kinds of interactions as we travel provides insights into how to negotiate and fulfill our strategic outcomes.

As I walk out of the Monrovia airport, a brightly smiling woman adorned in glowing orange from head to toe sells me a SIM card for my phone for USD $5. I hand her five U.S. dollars. I send a text message to my family to let them know I arrived safely. While walking, texting, and looking for my driver, I nearly trip over a woman relieving herself, I see kids selling drinking water, and I pass men my age who by Liberian standards are statistically in their final years. Using my phone to send a text message home makes the foreign seem familiar, but watching my kids' peers sell water makes the same place seem foreign.

After a decent night of sleep, I go for a morning run along the muddy streets by my hotel. I keep passing children carrying buckets of water on their heads from the nearby well. Breakfast at the hotel where I stay occurs at a large dining room table where guests are served two runny eggs, a hot dog, one piece of plain white bread, and a cup of instant coffee. On this particular morning, the breakfast table includes U.N. consultants from India and Sweden, an economist from the United States, some American business professionals, and a British physician.

I begin talking with the American businesswoman seated next to me. She works for a U.S. firm that sells baby food. She tells me this is her fifth trip to Monrovia in the last two years. After her first trip, she convinced her firm there was a growing market for baby food in Liberia, particularly among the many Liberians who were coming back after living abroad during the fifteen-year war. While overseas, these Liberians had seen the nutritional benefits and convenience of baby food and they were sure they could convince their fellow Liberians to buy it as well. The company shipped several containers full of baby food. The kinds of food sent were carefully selected based on market research of the Liberian diet, but the company used the same packaging used in the United States—a label with a picture of a baby on it. The company launched its product with lots of promotions including free samples for parents to try with their kids, but very few people picked up the samples, and even fewer purchased the baby food, despite it being introduced at a very low price. Sales of the baby food flopped in Liberia until the company suddenly realized African grocery distributors usually place pictures of the contents on their labels. Therefore, marketing a jar with a baby on the front didn't sell. Oops!

Hearing her story, the white-haired British doctor sitting across from us chimes in with a story of his own. He begins to tell us how he shipped several crates of medicine from Britain six months ago, but it still hasn't arrived in Liberia. He called and e-mailed the Monrovia shipyard from London every couple of days for the last few months and was continually told the shipment hadn't arrived yet. Once he reached Monrovia, he went to the dock almost daily to inquire whether his shipment had arrived. Each time he was told, "Come back tomorrow. It will definitely be on the next ship."

But it never is. He is beginning to think he'll never see the medical supplies, and the value of his brief sojourn in Liberia is becoming seriously undermined by not having them. He muses that it now seems a waste of time for him to have come.

I go on to share a couple of my own cultural mishaps and we talk about how easy it is to laugh at these things in retrospect, but at the time, the frustration and financial cost involved is anything but a laughing matter. Our breakfast conversation is a reminder of the many challenges that come with leading cross-culturally. And in a few minutes, I am about to discover that reality again myself.

One of the key objectives for my trip to Liberia is to decide whether we should include a Liberian school, Madison College (pseudonym), in the multitiered partnership we were developing throughout the country. Our primary organizational contact in Liberia is Moses, a catalytic Liberian who is leading an effort to rebuild the Liberian educational system after the war. Moses is the eldest of his father's eighty-five children and the son of his father's first wife. That makes him the highest-ranking member of his family now that his father is dead. Moses is short and stocky, and he carries himself like a tribal chief. He consistently cautioned our team against working with Madison College. He was concerned about the integrity and ethics of the president of the school, Dr. Jones. This morning, Moses and I are visiting Dr. Harris, who is another key leader in Monrovia. Dr. Harris has done a lot of work with Dr. Jones and Madison College. Dr. Harris is a tall, stately looking man who remains behind his desk while we talk, sitting rigid and straight in a navy blue suit.

Drawing on my value for direct communication, soon after we get through the perfunctory introductions, Dr. Harris mentions that he sometimes teaches at Madison. I take that as my cue. Notice our dialogue:

Dave: How do you like teaching at Madison, Dr. Harris? Is it a good school?

Dr. Harris: Oh, it's a great joy for me to teach there. The students are so eager to learn.

Dave: And how about Dr. Jones? What's he like as a leader?

Notice that while being direct, I am trying to ask open-ended questions, an approach that usually works well for me at home.

Dr. Harris: Madison is a very good school. Dr. Jones has been there for a long time, since before the war.

I can see my open-ended questions aren't getting me very far. My time with Dr. Harris is limited. I need his honest assessment of Dr. Jones, so I decide to go for it.

Dave: Sorry if what I'm about to ask is uncomfortable, Dr. Harris. But I've heard some concerns about Dr. Jones and his leadership. I'm not looking for unnecessary details. But we're considering a partnership with Dr. Jones and Madison College. This partnership would result in a high level of investment from our university. Might you be able to give me any perspective on these criticisms I keep hearing?

Dr. Harris: It would be very good for the students if you partner with Madison College. Our schools have nothing here. The war destroyed everything. It would be very, very good. Please come.

I'm not entirely clueless. I can see what is going on, but I don't have time for what feels like game playing to me. I come at it again.

Dave: Yes, that's why I'm here. But I wonder what you can tell me about Dr. Jones specifically. Would you feel good about endorsing him to us as a significant partner?

Dr. Harris: It's really quite amazing the school survived the war. I mean, of course they had to shut down for a while. The rebel soldiers overtook all of Monrovia. But they were one of the first places to reopen. They have very good people there.

Dave: And you feel good about the way Dr. Jones is leading there?

Dr. Harris: Dr. Jones has done many good things. We've been friends for many years. Actually, we were classmates together in primary school. It would be very good for you to help Madison. I can introduce him to you if you like.

As we walk away from the meeting, I turn quickly to assure Moses: "Moses. I don't want you to think I don't trust the validity of your concerns about Dr. Jones. It's just that it was important for me to get his input. But that doesn't mean I'm discounting your reservations."

Fortunately, Moses has learned to talk to a bottom-line American like me in a way that I get it. He replies,

> Don't you see, Dave?! Don't you see?! Of course he wasn't going to tell you his concerns about Dr. Jones. You should never have asked him that, especially not with me there. He would never speak disparagingly about him in front of another Liberian brother to a complete stranger from the States. They grew up together! What did you expect him to say?

I shoot back, "The truth! That's what. He doesn't need to give me gory details. But if he is aware of these improprieties Dr. Jones keeps being accused of, I expect him to at least encourage me to explore my concerns further. If someone asked me about a childhood friend I knew was embezzling money, I'd tell the truth!"

Moses explains that Dr. Harris may have delved into this with me a bit if we had been alone. He says, "But it would be shameful to him and me both if Dr. Harris had criticized his childhood friend in front of me to you. And he's teaching there. Talking about this like that would bring shame to him. You never should have asked him that. Never!"

I wasn't totally blind to the cross-cultural and interpersonal dynamics involved. But I was at an impasse in getting some key information I needed to move forward. Usually, I can make my way through these kinds of conflicts when interacting with individuals from similar cultural contexts as me. But the interpersonal skills and persuasive strategies I use intuitively at home were ineffective with these Liberian leaders. This is where cultural intelligence comes in. It helps us effectively to adapt our leadership strategies when working with individuals from different cultural backgrounds. Later, I'll show you how it helped me move forward in this situation.

Relevance to Leaders

Perhaps the world is not so flat after all, especially when you consider Liberia is closer to the norm for many places in the world than the exception. The discrepancies are clear. And more of us move in and out of these stark cultural contrasts almost as easily as we surf from one channel to another while watching television. The ease with which we encounter so many cultural differences in a twenty-four-hour period can lead us to underestimate the chasm of difference between one culture and the next—whether it's Grand Rapids and Monrovia, France and Germany, or Starbucks and Shell. Friedman's idea of a flattening world is very appropriate when applied to the growing competition and opportunities in emerging economies. But we need to resist applying the notion of a flat world to suggesting that we can do business as usual wherever we go.

In fact, 90 percent of leading executives from sixty-eight countries named cross-cultural leadership as the top management challenge for the next century.[4] It used to be that worldwide travel and cross-cultural interaction were largely reserved for government ambassadors and high-level executives from massive multinational corporations like IBM and McDonald's. Today, almost every leader engages in a myriad of cross-cultural interactions. For some, that means traveling through passport control to the fascinating worlds of new foods and languages. For others, cross-cultural encounters are as close as their e-mail in-box, the person on the other side of the cubicle, or the diverse students scattered across campus.

Leaders across every profession are being propelled into a culturally rich and diverse challenge. Both an intuitive sense of leadership and expertise in one's field continue to be valuable leadership assets, but they are no longer enough to manage today's diverse opportunities. Hospital presidents are overseeing healthcare professionals who are treating patients from numerous cultural backgrounds. Military officers are giving orders to eighteen-year-olds that if not carried out well will show up as international incidents on BBC and CNN. And business executives from Fortune 500 companies to entrepreneurial start-ups are facing growing pressure to recruit and lead talent to sell and produce products across international borders.

Today's professional may easily encounter fifteen different cultural contexts in a single day. By culture, I simply mean any group of people who have a shared way of seeing and making sense of the world. A much higher degree of adaptability is needed to work within all of the cultures we encounter. In addition to working across many national and ethnic cultures, professionals have to navigate various organizational contexts. And perhaps most important, effective leaders need a strong awareness of their own cultural identity. It's easy to become overwhelmed by it all! Without an ability to adapt to a growing number of cultures, leaders and their organizations often become obsolete. But it doesn't have to be that way. Cultural intelligence is an ability uniquely suited for the barrage of cultures faced by most contemporary leaders. Rather than expecting individuals to master all the norms of the various cultures encountered, cultural intelligence helps a leader develop an overall repertoire and perspective that results in more effective leadership.

Executives report that leading *without* cultural intelligence results in increased time to get the job done, heightened travel time and costs, growing frustration and confusion, poor job performance, decreased revenues, poor working relationships at home and abroad, and lost opportunities.[5] Therefore, the most pressing reasons leaders need cultural intelligence is to understand a diversifying customer base, to manage diverse and cross-border teams, to recruit and develop cross-cultural talent, to adapt their leadership style, and to demonstrate genuine respect for all kinds of people. A few words need to be said about each of these reasons before more thoroughly unpacking CQ.

WHY CQ?

Nearly 90 percent of leading executives from sixty-eight countries named cross-cultural leadership as the top management challenge for the next century.[3] Most contemporary leaders encounter dozens of different cultures daily. It's impossible to master all the norms and values of each culture, but effective leadership *does* require some adaptation in approach and strategy. The most pressing issues executives identify for why CQ is needed are to:

- Understand diverse customers.

- Manage diverse teams.

- Recruit and develop cross-cultural talent.

- Adapt leadership style.

- Demonstrate respect.

Understand Diverse Customers

The days of identifying a single target customer are long gone for most organizations. Most nonprofit and corporate leaders are serving customers whose tastes, behaviors, and assumptions are not only different but are often in conflict with one another. Putting a picture of pureed carrots on the label of a baby food jar might reduce sales in a U.S. market, but doing so in Liberia suddenly made the same product more marketable.

The proportion of revenue coming from overseas markets is expected to jump by an average of 30 to 50 percent over the next three to five years. Growing numbers of companies are like Coca-Cola, which sells more of its product in Japan than it sells in the United States. By 2003, 56 percent of U.S. franchise operators (e.g., Dunkin' Donuts or KFC) were in markets outside of the United States.[6] The demand from emerging markets is seen as the most critical factor facing global businesses. The spending power of China and India is increasing at an enormous rate. The *Economist's CEO Briefing* reported that: "The number of households earning more than USD $5,000 annually will more than double over the next five years in China, and will triple in India."[7] Even the recent economic crisis is not expected to alter these trends.

Executives surveyed cite understanding customers across various contexts as the greatest of all the global leadership challenges. There's really no such thing as a uniform global culture to which we market. Today's organization and its leaders must be both local and global, or "glocal," in understanding and serving customers.

Manage Diverse Teams

The task of managing a diversified and dispersed workforce at home and internationally is another major test of leadership. Fostering good communication and building trust have always been two seminal issues in leadership, but learning how to do so among a culturally diverse staff is a whole new challenge. Human resource policies, motivational strategies, and performance reviews may need to be adapted for various cultural groups represented among your team members. In addition, tapping into a global workforce often means outsourcing service to India and manufacturing to China. But knowing how to measure the costs, benefits, and appropriate expectations involved with these kinds of opportunities is fraught with complexity.

Furthermore, growing numbers of the workforce in most companies are expected to work across international borders. Individuals who used to manage a product line in one plant now find themselves living on airplanes and talking with teams and clients scattered around the world.[8] Leaders are needed who can help teams form a local identity while still retaining the values of the organization as a whole. Cultural intelligence is needed to achieve the right blend of flexibility and rigidity in global management.

Recruit and Develop Cross-Cultural Talent

Cultural intelligence is also needed to address the challenge of recruiting, developing, and retaining cross-cultural talent. Up and coming leaders in emerging economies have many options at their disposal and they're seeking firms and executives who demonstrate culturally intelligent practice. Katherine Tsang, CEO of Standard Chartered Bank China, responded to this challenge by creating what she calls a superhighway for attracting and retaining young, globally minded leaders. Her mantra to her team is "Go places!"—a double entendre for working with a global network of affiliates and growing a personal portfolio in global leadership. Tsang identifies the race for good talent as one of the most pressing reasons her company must become more culturally astute.[9]

Executives recognize the need to recruit the right personnel because 16 to 40 percent of all managers given foreign assignments

as expatriates end them early. Nearly 99 percent of these early ter-
minations are the result of cultural issues, not job skills. The cost
of each failed expatriate assignment has been estimated anywhere
from USD $250,000 to more than USD $1.25 million when you
include expenses associated with moving, downtime, and a myriad
of other direct and indirect costs.[10]

Cultural intelligence is becoming a growing necessity even
for employees who never take an extended assignment overseas.
A growing number of employees are expected to take short trips
overseas to work with colleagues and customers or to work with
international clients from home. Organizations practicing cultural
intelligence are more likely to recruit and retain the talent needed
to meet these demands.[11]

Adapt Leadership Style

When leading across different cultures, we also need cultural intelligence to adapt our leadership style. One time I went to my company's regional office in Prague to join a two-day meeting with all
of our midlevel managers from Eastern Europe. After the two-day
meeting, our regional director asked me who among the group
did I perceive to be the most promising up-and-coming leaders.
Without hesitation, I named three individuals who struck me as
having "leader" written all over them. He laughed and said, "I
thought you'd say that. Their charisma and initiative would probably be a huge asset in the United States, but it's a liability here."
He went on to tell me whom he thought were the most promising
leaders—individuals who had barely hit my radar. Two years later,
one of the individuals he identified was the new regional director
and performed with excellence.

Just as individuals possess varying views and beliefs about
preferred styles of leadership, cultures as a whole have varying
preferences for certain leadership approaches. A study across
sixty-two countries, "Global Leadership and Organizational

Behavior Effectiveness," found that national and organizational cultures influenced the kind of leadership found to be acceptable and effective by people within that culture. For example, a participative leadership style where managers involve others in decision making was viewed as an essential way of working among most German leaders and organizations. However, this same style was viewed as a weakness among many firms and leaders from Saudi Arabia, where authoritative leadership was perceived as a strength.[12]

Many of these cultural preferences for leadership style are related to the values embraced by a culture as a whole. This is a relationship we'll explore more fully throughout the book. For now, the point is to see the importance of having the knowledge, motivation, and flexibility to enact the appropriate leadership style in any given situation.[13]

Demonstrate Respect

A competitive advantage, increased profits, and global expansion are central to why many of us are interested in cultural intelligence; however, most of us would readily agree we're also interested in behaving in a more respectful, humanizing manner to the people we meet throughout our work. Cultural intelligence can help us to become more benevolent in how we view those who see the world differently from us. The *desire* to treat other people with honor and respect doesn't automatically mean our *behavior* comes across as dignifying and kind. There are various adaptations necessary in order to ensure people experience respect and honor from us. This kind of posture requires capabilities included in cultural intelligence.

These five reasons for cultural intelligence—understanding customers, managing personnel, recruiting talent, adapting leadership style, and communicating respect—are the most consistent reasons identified by leading executives across the world. These needs will continue to surface throughout the book as we more fully discover how to lead with cultural intelligence.

Cultural Intelligence vs. Other Intercultural Approaches

Although most of us need little convincing that leadership is a multicultural challenge, what does the cultural intelligence approach uniquely offer? Theories, books, and training on diversity and on global leadership abound. Some include cultural sensitivity tests that are well known and widely used. A great deal of this material informs how we've conceptualized, researched, and applied CQ to the leadership context. However, there are a few important differences between CQ and other intercultural approaches. The distinctions are briefly noted here, several of which will resurface in the fuller description of cultural intelligence found in Chapter 2. The primary ways CQ differs from other leading approaches to global management are:

- *CQ is a meta-framework rooted in rigorous, academic research.* A key strength of the cultural intelligence concept is that it's a research-based, metaframework that synthesizes volumes of material and perspectives on cross-cultural leadership and diversity. The CQ measure has been tested across multiple samples, times, and cultures.
- *CQ is based on the multiple intelligences research.* Cultural intelligence is the only approach to cross-cultural leadership explicitly rooted in contemporary theories of intelligence. The four-dimensional model of CQ is directly connected to the four aspects of intelligence (motivational, cognitive, metacognitive, and behavioral) that have been broadly researched and applied around the world. CQ is a specific form of intelligence that helps individuals function effectively in multicultural situations.[14]

- *CQ is more than just knowledge.* The cultural intelligence approach goes beyond simply emphasizing cultural understanding. It also includes a leader's *personal* interests, strategic thinking, and resulting behavior in cross-cultural situations. Understanding the sociological differences in cultural beliefs, values, and behaviors is essential, but it is incomplete apart from also exploring the psychological dynamics involved as one person interacts with another.

- *CQ emphasizes learned capabilities more than personality traits.* Although it's helpful to understand how our predisposed personality influences our cross-cultural behavior (e.g., extroverts versus introverts) it can be paralyzing because personality is difficult to change. The emphasis of CQ, however, is on what any leader can do to *enhance* cultural intelligence through education, training, and experience. CQ is not fixed; rather it can develop and grow.

- *CQ is not culturally specific.* Finally, cultural intelligence is not specific to a particular culture. The emphasis is not on mastering all of the specific information and behavior needed for individual cultures. Instead, CQ focuses on developing an overall repertoire of understanding, skills, and behaviors for making sense of the barrage of cultures we encounter daily.[15]

The relevance of these distinctions of CQ will be elevated in Chapter 2 in more thoroughly describing the cultural intelligence model. Cultural intelligence offers leaders a realistic, practical skill set to meet the demands of leadership in today's fast-paced world.

Conclusion

Stop and look around you. How is culture shaping what's there? How is it shaping what you see? It is. I guarantee it. And the degree to which you can see it and adapt accordingly is critical.

I'm sitting in an airport right now. For a split second, I forgot where I was. And the familiarity of the scene around me did little to help. The Body Shop is right in front of me, the Disney Store is to my left, Starbucks is to my right, and the huge duty free shopping store is just around the corner. The guy next to me is typing away furiously on a Dell laptop. It's easy to see the familiar airport totem poles in Sydney, Sao Paulo, London, Hong Kong, Orlando, and Johannesburg and believe the world is flat in every way. In part, it is. You can order your grande, triple-shot, nonfat, vanilla, no-foam Starbucks latte in more than twenty-five countries of the world. And endless competitors offer their own versions of the same drink in many more places. But beware of thinking the same negotiating skills, sense of humor, and motivational techniques can be used indiscriminately with everyone and everywhere.

Leading in the twenty-first-century world means maneuvering the twists and turns of a multidimensional world. The continually shifting landscape of global leadership can be disorienting; experience and intuition alone are not enough. But cultural intelligence offers a way through the maze that's not only effective but also invigorating and fulfilling. Join a community of leaders across the world who are acquiring cultural intelligence to tap into the opportunities and results of leading across our rapidly globalizing world.

CHAPTER 2

YOU NEED A MAP FOR THE JOURNEY:

CQ OVERVIEW

If two American leaders go through identical training for an assignment in Brazil, they'll still have two very different experiences because they're two very different people. We all are.

Of all the ways cultural intelligence differs from other approaches to cross-cultural leadership, the fact that CQ is an *individual capability* is the most significant difference. We each have a different cultural intelligence quotient (CQ). Uniform training and strategies don't equal uniform performance.

Two weeks before I went to Monrovia, I was speaking about globalization with a group of leaders gathered at a large university in the United States. While I was there, I spent several hours one afternoon interviewing a group of business students who had just completed a ten-day study trip to India. Before our afternoon meeting, I began talking with one of the professors who participated in this trip. He was a fifty-two-year-old tenured business professor who had been at the university for seventeen years. Picture the stereotypical faculty member with ruffled hair, a tweed jacket, and the smell of a pipe. He began telling me his observations about the Indian business leaders they encountered. He said, "They're all a bunch of damn chauvinistic racists! Every last one of them. Really! Show me an Indian business leader who isn't!"

A few minutes later, I was talking with some of the students about their observations from the trip to India. Drew, a blond-haired, blue-eyed nineteen-year-old sophomore business major, was the first one to speak up. He looked like he had just walked in from playing a foursome on the golf course. He had this to say about the company where he spent the most time in Bangalore: "I'm really having to rethink my views on whether *team* leadership is the only effective way to run a company. The people there seem to thrive despite all the formality, titles, and top-down approach."

I was far more encouraged by Drew's interest in rethinking his own assumptions about leadership styles than I was by the dogmatic statement made by the business professor. Is it really fair to say every business leader from a population of more than 1 billion people is chauvinistic and racist? We might have expected the bias connected with the previous statements to be reversed. Surely seasoned professors are better at cross-cultural sensitivity than nineteen-year-old frat guys! These statements raise an age-old perplexing question: Why is it some leaders easily and effectively adapt their views and behaviors cross-culturally and others don't? Which kind of leader are you?

Education and international experience play a strong role in developing our level of cultural intelligence, but they don't guarantee success.[1] I've met business leaders and government officials who have lived for decades overseas yet they demonstrate very little ability to see beyond their cultural blinders. And I've met other leaders living abroad, sometimes with minimal international experience, who are extremely adept at moving in and out of various cultural contexts and situations while still remaining true to who they are. What makes the difference? What abilities and skills consistently yield results in effective cross-cultural leadership? Answering these questions is at the core of the cultural intelligence approach.

WHAT IS CQ?

Cultural intelligence (CQ) is the capability to function effectively across national, ethnic, and organizational cultures.[2] It is:

- A four-dimensional model

- A four-step cycle

- Different from emotional intelligence
- A repertoire of skills
- An inside-out approach

The rest of the chapter provides a fuller definition of cultural intelligence, which builds on the distinctions referenced at the end of Chapter 1 (including that CQ is research based, is more than just knowledge, empahsizes learner capabilities, and is not culturally specific).

A Four-Dimensional Model

Cultural intelligence is a four-dimensional framework rooted in many years of research on intelligence and cross-cultural interaction. All four dimensions are essential in order to gain the benefits of CQ. The four dimensions are CQ drive, CQ knowledge, CQ strategy, and CQ action, usually referenced in the research as motivational CQ, cognitive CQ, metacognitive CQ, and behavioral CQ (see Figure 2-1). Researchers Linn Van Dyne and Soon Ang have also suggested subdimensions for each one of these four dimensions as noted in Figure 2-1.[3]

Figure 2-1. The Four Dimensional Model of Cultural Intelligence

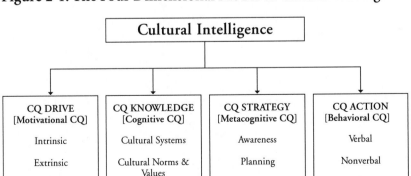

Cultural Intelligence			
CQ DRIVE [Motivational CQ]	**CQ KNOWLEDGE** [Cognitive CQ]	**CQ STRATEGY** [Metacognitive CQ]	**CQ ACTION** [Behavioral CQ]
Intrinsic	Cultural Systems	Awareness	Verbal
Extrinsic	Cultural Norms & Values	Planning	Nonverbal
Self-Efficacy		Checking	Speech Acts

CQ Drive: Showing Interest, Confidence, and Drive to Adapt Cross-Culturally

CQ drive, the motivational dimension of CQ, is the leader's level of interest, drive, and energy to adapt cross-culturally. Do you have the confidence and drive to work through the challenges and conflicts that inevitably accompany cross-cultural work? The ability to be personally engaged and to persevere through cross-cultural challenges is one of the most novel and important aspects of cultural intelligence. We cannot simply *assume* people are interested and motivated to adjust to cultural differences. Employees often approach diversity training apathetically and do it just because it's required. Personnel headed to international assignments are often more concerned about moving and adjusting their families overseas than they are about developing cultural understanding. Without ample motivation, there's little point in spending time and money on cross-cultural training.

CQ drive includes three sub-imensions: *intrinsic motivation* —the degree to which you derive enjoyment from culturally diverse situations; *extrinsic motivation*—the tangible benefits you gain from culturally diverse experiences; and *self-efficacy*—the confidence that you will be effective in a cross-cultural encounter.[4] All three of these motivational dynamics play a role in how leaders approach cross-cultural situations.[5]

CQ Knowledge: Understanding Cross-Cultural Issues and Differences

CQ knowledge, the cognitive dimension of the CQ research, refers to the leader's knowledge about culture and its role in shaping how business is done. Do you understand the way culture shapes thinking and behavior? It also includes your overall understanding of how cultures vary from one another. CQ knowledge includes two subdimensions: *cultural systems* and *cultural norms and values.*[6]

Cultural systems are the ways societies organize themselves to meet the basic needs of their members. For example, every nation has cultural systems for how its members distribute products and services or for how they mate and raise their children. Understanding how a family system works might seem unnecessary but it becomes critically relevant when you're trying to develop human resource policies for employees who are expected to care for the senior members of their extended family. The other subdimension of CQ knowledge, cultural norms and values, refers to the varying ways cultures approach issues such as time, authority, and relationships. The value a culture places on time and relationships becomes highly germane when an American is trying to get a signed contract from a potential affiliate in China or Saudi Arabia, where different norms shape leaders' expectations.

CQ knowledge is the dimension most often emphasized in many approaches to intercultural competency. For example, a large and growing training and consulting industry focuses on teaching leaders this kind of cultural knowledge. Although valuable, however, the knowledge coming from CQ knowledge has to be combined with the other three dimensions of CQ or its relevance to the real demands of leadership is questionable and potentially detrimental.

CQ Strategy: Strategizing and Making Sense of Culturally Diverse Experiences

CQ strategy, also known as metacognitive CQ, is the leader's ability to strategize when crossing cultures. Can we slow down the RPMs long enough to carefully observe what's going on inside the minds of ourselves and others? It's the ability to draw upon our cultural understanding to solve culturally complex problems. CQ strategy helps a leader use cultural knowledge to plan an appropriate strategy, accurately interpret what's going on, and check to see if expectations are accurate or need revision.

The three subdimensions of CQ strategy are *awareness, planning,* and *checking*.[7] Awareness means being in tune with what's going on in ourselves and others. Planning is taking time to prepare for a cross-cultural encounter—anticipating how to approach the people, topic, and situation. Checking is monitoring our interactions to see if our plans and expectations were appropriate. It is also comparing what we expected with our actual experience. CQ strategy emphasizes strategy and is the lynchpin between understanding cultural issues and actually being able to use our understanding to be more effective.

CQ Action: Changing Verbal and Nonverbal *Actions* Appropriately When Interacting Cross–Culturally

CQ action, the behavioral dimension of CQ, is the leader's ability to *act* appropriately in a range of cross-cultural situations. Can we effectively accomplish our performance goals in different cultural situations? One of the most important aspects of CQ action is knowing when to adapt to another culture and when *not* to do so. A person with high CQ learns which actions will and will not enhance effectiveness and acts on that understanding. Thus, CQ action involves flexible actions tailored to specific cultural contexts.

The subdimensions of CQ action are *verbal actions, nonverbal actions,* and *speech acts*—the exact words and phrases we use when we communicate specific types of messages.[8] These are the three kinds of behaviors where there is the greatest need to adapt to cultural norms. Although the demands of today's intercultural settings make it impossible to master all the dos and don'ts of various cultures, there are certain behaviors that should be modified when we interact with different cultures. For example, Westerners need to learn the importance of carefully studying business cards presented by those from most Asian contexts. Also, some basic verbal and nonverbal behaviors enhance the extent to which we are seen as being effective by others. As an example, the verbal tone (e.g., loud versus soft) in which words are spoken can convey different meanings across cultures. Almost every approach to cross-cultural work has insisted on the importance of flexibility. With CQ action, we now have a way of exploring how to enhance our flexibility.

Chapters 3 to 7 will more thoroughly explore each of these dimensions. Research, examples, and best practices will be offered to move toward gaining the capabilities represented by these four dimensions.

The Cultural Intelligence Scale (CQS) measures competency in each of the four dimensions.[9] Through a series of questions, you receive four scores, one for each dimension of cultural intelligence. By averaging these four scores together, you can estimate your overall CQ. Two different CQ assessments are available, both of which have relevance for improving leadership effectiveness. One is a self-report assessment and the other is a peer-report assessment. The self-assessment provides a profile of how you view yourself in the four dimensions of cultural intelligence. The peer-assessment asks you to identify three to five peers who can answer a few questions on your behalf. In return, you receive a composite of how your peers view you in the four dimensions of cultural intelligence. The two kinds of assessments are most valuable when used together so you can compare your self-assessment with how others perceive your cultural intelligence.[10] Visit the website http://www.cq-portal.com for more information about these assessments.

There are a variety of ways to apply the four dimensions of cultural intelligence to leadership. They can be used as four areas to assess individuals you're considering for a cross-cultural assignment. They can also serve as four categories for diversity training or for a leader's personal development plan. And the four dimensions can be used as a four-step cycle for developing cultural intelligence both over the long haul and in case-by-case situations. This four-step cycle, as portrayed in Figure 2-2, is the primary application used in this book. Although the four dimensions of cultural

Figure 2-2. The Four-Step Cycle of Cultural Intelligence

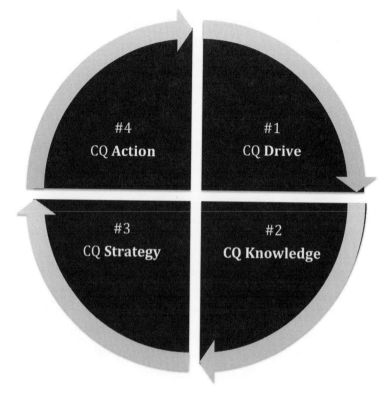

intelligence don't always develop in one particular order, Linn Van Dyne and Soon Ang suggest it can be helpful to think about the four dimensions of CQ as four steps toward increased CQ.[11] It might look something like this:

- Step 1: CQ drive (motivational dimension) gives us the energy and self-confidence to pursue the needed understanding and planning necessary for a particular cross-cultural assignment.
- Step 2: CQ knowledge (cognitive dimension) provides us with an understanding of basic cultural issues that are relevant to this assignment.

- Step 3: CQ strategy (metacognitive dimension) allows us to draw on our cultural understanding so we can plan and interpret what's going on in this situation.
- Step 4: CQ action (behavioral dimension) provides us with the ability to engage in effective, flexible leadership for this task.

As people respond to our cross-cultural behavior (Step 4), either positively or negatively, the cycle comes back full circle to CQ drive (Step 1). Feedback from others offers a motivational source for continuing our development of cultural intelligence. As the cycle repeats itself, our overall cultural intelligence has the potential to keep developing and growing. Cultural intelligence is not a static ability. It continues to morph and develop as we go about our daily work.

The four-step cycle offers a promising way to move CQ from theory to practice. We can continually move through the four steps at a macro level in thinking about our overall leadership across a diversity of situations. And we can work through the loop even on the fly while engaging in cross-cultural conversations and negotiations. You don't have to be a pro at understanding everything about working with a Chinese affiliate on a new project. But run the project through these four steps as a way to get started.

1. What's it going to take to motivate you?
2. What do you need to know?
3. What's your plan?
3. What behaviors should you adapt?

Nobody ever gets to the end of this journey of cultural intelligence. We just keep working these steps through lots of different scenarios and contexts. As we do so, we'll continually get better. That's what we're after — increasing our effectiveness in our work across the global context. We'll utilize this four-step progression as we walk through the four dimensions of cultural intelligence in Chapters 3 to 7.

CQ Is Different from EQ

CQ is an additional form of intelligence. We all know what IQ is—a measurement of one's intellectual capabilities. In recent years, we've also seen the significance of EQ, or emotional intelligence—one's ability to effectively lead socially and emotionally. Technical expertise isn't enough. Leaders need to be able to work with people. Emotional intelligence helps assess the degree to which we're able to perceive, assess, and manage the emotions of ourselves and others.[12] Research shows that leaders with strong emotional intelligence are more effective, but it's not a reliable indicator of whether that effectiveness is sustained outside one's own cultural context. Cultural intelligence picks up where emotional intelligence leaves off. Cultural intelligence helps us learn how to work effectively with people who come from different cultural orientations. It helps ensure leadership effectiveness across cultural borders.[13]

Shelly is another one of the students from the university who went to Bangalore, India, on the ten-day study trip. The day we met, Shelly was wearing heels, a black suit, and her hair was pulled up in a knot. She offered warm, nonverbal affirmation whenever her peers spoke. It only took a few minutes of interaction with Shelly to see she would probably score pretty high on an EQ assessment. She was an excellent conversationalist and several times during the focus group meeting, Shelly not only responded to my questions but also found ways to draw in those students who had previously been sitting disengaged. Yet ironically, when I asked Shelly, "So what was the biggest challenge you faced when you were in Bangalore?" she replied, "Just getting people to talk with me. It was totally awkward. I tried everything I could think of and most of my conversations went nowhere. Even though they speak great English, we never seemed to get into real conversations."

Individuals who have a strong ability to empathize and relate to people in their own cultures might find the same empathetic and social skills get them nowhere when interacting with someone from a different cultural background. This can be extremely frustrating to someone like Shelly who usually finds social interaction natural. In contrast, some individuals with limited social skills at home might actually fare quite decently in another culture. So the books and training on emotional intelligence presume a level of familiarity with the culture of those with whom we interact and lead. This is why the additional capabilities represented by cultural intelligence are needed.

Whatever your CQ score, it's not fixed. Your cultural intelligence can be continually enhanced through education, interactions, and experience. A variety of experiences and methods can result in an increased CQ. Of course, the reverse is also true. One can actually become less culturally intelligent although that isn't as likely. As we walk through the four-step cycle of CQ in the chapters that follow, I've included research-based strategies to grow in each dimension of cultural intelligence.

The inevitable question gets raised over whether cultural intelligence is a matter of nature or nurture. Are some people just genetically inclined toward being more culturally intelligent? The answer is quite possibly yes. Just as some of us are more naturally oriented to be better runners, engineers, or musicians, so also some of us may be genetically inclined toward more flexible behavior cross-culturally. For example, the research finds that being an extrovert is correlated to some of the dimensions of cultural intelligence. There's also a positive relationship between being naturally conscientious and having higher CQ strategy; and the personality trait referred to as "openness," a general curiosity toward circumstances and the world, is positively related to all four dimensions of cultural intelligence.[14] So there are some interesting correlations between our personalities and cultural intelligence. However, the emphasis of cultural intelligence is that *through learning and interventions, everyone can become more culturally intelligent.* And just because someone might have natural talent at flexing his or her behavior in

33

cross-cultural situations, it's no guarantee he or she will be a culturally intelligent leader. Just as having natural genetics for running doesn't mean you'll be a marathon runner without training, the same is true here. It takes effort and work, but anyone can develop and nurture cultural intelligence.

A Repertoire of Skills

Let's say that the team from Spain is arriving in two hours, so there's little time to read up on Spanish culture right now. What should you do? Our busy lives simply don't allow us to become cultural experts about every culture with which we work. Cultural intelligence offers a more promising and realistic approach. According to researchers Maddy Janssens and Tineke Cappellen's study of global managers, a more broad-based approach for orienting professionals is needed. Their study validates the preferred *emphasis of cultural intelligence on developing an overall repertoire of skills and behaviors* that you can draw on when engaging in any cross-cultural interaction rather than expecting you to master all the ins and outs of each culture.[15]

The broader approach taken by cultural intelligence is what initially drew me to the research and model. Much of my own work has required lots of short-term, episodic travel. I was convinced culture was a significant force in how we did our work, but I felt paralyzed by the unrealistic notion of becoming a cultural expert on all the different people and places encountered.

Now there is a place for more specific and intensified understanding about certain cultures. When it became clear I was going to be responsible for leading our work in Liberia, I knew I needed to grow my understanding of Liberia's historical and cultural background. It would have been careless for me to just rely on a general understanding of cultures to do my work effectively. But I also wasn't starting from zero. Even though I had never been to Liberia nor spent any time studying the culture, a growing measure of cultural intelligence helped me know what kinds of information to find out and the kinds of questions to ask. I've already demonstrated that my previous experiences and understanding didn't keep me from making mistakes. And I have plenty more mistakes like those to share. But thankfully, our mistakes can be one of the greatest ways to grow our cultural intelligence. In fact, part of being more culturally intelligent is embracing the idea that cross-cultural conflict is inevitable and provides an opportunity for personal and professional growth.

You too will have certain organizational, generational, and socio-ethnic cultures where you need to gain more specific understanding. But the primary emphasis of the cultural intelligence approach is to develop a skill set that can be applied to all kinds of cultural situations. Although some initial reading and training in cultural intelligence can jump-start your growth in cultural intelligence, we continue to add to our repertoire for culturally intelligent leadership all through our career. The four-step model applies equally to novice travelers and to well-seasoned multinational executives.

An Inside-Out Approach

There's little hope we can adapt our cross-cultural behavior in any kind of sustained way unless we actually change the way we see our fellow citizens around the world. We have to move beyond behavior modification approaches wherein we *pretend* to be respectful and move toward becoming leaders who *genuinely respect* and value people from different cultural backgrounds. This seems to be the most significant factor determining whether a leader truly behaves with cultural intelligence. All the diversity awareness programs and creative cross-cultural simulations are pointless if we don't actually change the way we view people from within.

Education is by far the most familiar antidote used by organizations that want to address the challenges of cultural diversity.

When facing the issues that surface as a result of cultural differences, the default is to get everyone together and teach them about things like sexual harassment or cultural taboos. As one who is highly invested in the education field, I'm not going to be disparaging the value of good teaching and learning that leads to more effective cross-cultural work. But some of our findings about what occurs as a result of an overemphasis on education in this arena are less encouraging.[16]

One of the complaints I often hear from employees as they assess diversity training is that it made little difference to what actually occurred in the workplace. Sure, it was helpful to remind men they shouldn't refer to their female colleagues as "the girls" and it was informative to see how a Chinese colleague might be more reticent to provide critical feedback upward than a colleague from Australia. But if a guy doesn't view his female colleagues with respect or if an Aussie leader still sees her Chinese affiliate as needing to "learn to speak up," has much been accomplished? Don't get me wrong. Getting people to use respectful language is a good start. But something more is needed.

One study reviewed a company that had developed a full-orbed diversity training program to help deal with the abysmal morale occurring throughout the organization. Thousands of dollars later and after lots of diversity training workshops, little had changed. Only through a more in-depth analysis did it surface that the CEO of the organization, a former U.S. Marine, was extremely prejudiced against overweight employees. He viewed an overweight employee as evidence of an undisciplined, lazy worker. He and his peers had been through countless hours of interventions and training for enhancing their respect of women and people of color. But the core issue wasn't being addressed.[17] The cultural intelligence approach with an emphasis on the *personal* attributes of leadership may have revealed this problem sooner.

Becoming culturally intelligent doesn't imply turning our backs on our own cultural backgrounds and preferences. But it does mean we have to do more than simply change the way we talk to our colleagues who look different from us, whether that's a difference in size, gender, color, or otherwise. And we have to go beyond merely planning a diversity-training month once a year. The entire way we view one another may need to be transformed. Much more guidance about what that looks like will be offered throughout the rest of the book. Cultural intelligence is a transformative model of cross-cultural behavior and leadership rather than a model built primarily on behavior modification strategies.

Conclusion

Some individuals have high CQ and others don't, but almost everyone can become more culturally intelligent by working the four-step cycle. Cultural intelligence is uniquely suited for the barrage of cultural situations facing today's leaders. It includes a set of competencies needed by leaders in every field. Without it, leaders risk running their careers and their organizations into obsolescence. But leaders who commit to improving the ways they think, plan, and act through cross-cultural situations have an unusual edge for navigating the fascinating terrain of our curvy, multidimensional world.

Cultural intelligence is a learned capability that builds on the other forms of intelligence needed by today's leaders. Just as leaders can grow in their social, emotional, and technical competence, they can grow in their ability to effectively lead across various ethnic and organizational cultures. As leaders move through the four-step cycle of cultural intelligence—CQ drive, CQ knowledge, CQ strategy, and CQ action—they gain a repertoire of perspectives, skills, and behaviors for use as they move in and out of the fast-paced world of globalization. True cultural intelligence stems from within and transforms the way we lead at home and across the globe. The four-step cycle of cultural intelligence moves us forward.

Part II

How Do I Become More Culturally Intelligent?

CHAPTER 3

WHET YOUR APPETITE: CQ DRIVE (STEP 1)

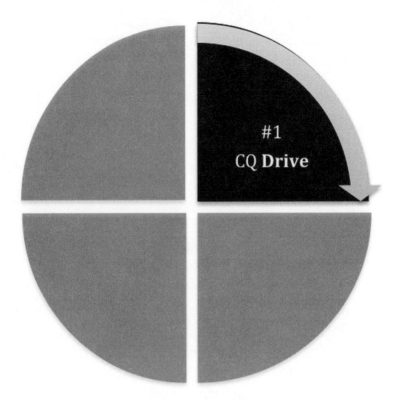

STEP 1: CQ DRIVE: What's my motivation?

Showing interest, confidence, and drive to adapt cross-culturally

Profile of a leader with high CQ drive:	Leaders with high CQ drive are motivated to learn and adapt to new and diverse cultural settings. Their confidence in their adaptive abilities is likely to influence the way they perform in multicultural situations.

confess. I'm totally energized by cross-cultural encounters. Put me in a room full of people and the internationals in the room draw me like a magnet. Ask me where I want to eat and I'll choose something ethnically exotic. Book me on an international flight and my adrenaline starts pumping. I love to blaze the streets of a new place, savor the local food, roam the neighborhoods, and shop at the local markets. My international work has been well served by my insatiable wanderlust. But sometimes it's gotten me into trouble. Not all of my colleagues and staff have shared my love for all things cross-cultural. I was at a conference in Bangkok with a group of colleagues and I told them that I knew a great little place where we could grab some local tribal food. My suggestion was almost unanimously vetoed and much to my chagrin, we ended up at Tony Roma's for steak and ribs. Another time I enthusiastically told a couple of my travel companions that our partner in Mexico had decided to move our upcoming meeting to an outlying village rather than in Mexico City. "You've got to be kidding," one replied, and the other said, "Why waste all that time getting out there when we could just meet at the comfortable hotel where we always stay?"

I'm learning not to assume everyone will be as excited as I am about venturing into a new place. We have varying levels of motivation and drive for working across cultures and that's okay. Some of us love to travel and experience different places and people. Others prefer to never leave home; however, no leader can escape working in a global context today. Even without an innate passion for all things diverse, there are some simple ways to grow in your motivation for cross-cultural work. CQ drive—the motivational dimension of cultural intelligence—is one of the most important features of the cultural intelligence model. Many organizations jump into offering training about cross-cultural differences without first assessing whether employees are motivated to be more effective cross-culturally. This is one of the reasons diversity-training programs often fail. If employees aren't motivated to change the ways they relate with various groups, the training might be a waste of time. There's a direct correlation between an individual's level of motivation to adapt cross-culturally and follow-on performance.

Sometimes our reluctant motivation stems from something in our past experience. Take Wendy, for example, a no-nonsense, thirty-seven-year-old professional who grew up in an upper-middle-class home in upstate New York. She went to Cornell University, got her MBA at Harvard, and spent seven years climbing the corporate ladder in New York City. She walks with a confidence not easily missed by her straight posture, her warm but self-assured smile, and her articulate speech. But throughout her studies and work, she had always been a big sister to kids in underprivileged neighborhoods. Five years ago, Wendy made a drastic career shift and accepted a job as the CEO of a nonprofit organization focused on helping children at risk.

Throughout its fifteen-year history, Wendy's organization has been focused primarily on serving children in underresourced communities throughout the United States and Canada. Last year, the board charged Wendy with expanding its work into Central America. Wendy has resisted expanding into Central America for fear the organization will lose focus, but she agreed to look into it. When I met Wendy, she had spent the previous six months reading everything she could about the issues facing children in places like Mexico City, Managua, and San Salvador. She read lots about the cultural issues throughout the region and she was even shoring up her Spanish. When Wendy agreed to meet me as part of my research on culturally intelligent leadership in nonprofits, she was two weeks away from making her first trip to Central America on behalf of the organization.

Wendy said, "Put me with a group of leaders on the south side of Chicago or among a bunch of community activists in rural Saskatchewan and I know what to do. I have a clear sense of how we can serve the needs of children there. But even after all the reading and learning I've been doing, I still don't have a clue how we should adapt our programs to meet the needs of kids down there." Frankly, I was encouraged that she wasn't overly confident about how their organization's programs would work there, but I observed an overall reticence to how Wendy talked about this expansion into Central America.

Then I asked Wendy, "So are you looking forward to this trip?" She replied, "Ah—you know what it's like. Travel gets old pretty fast. But it will be fine. My only visits down there have been a couple of beach vacations in Mexico and Costa Rica." I continued, "But how about this whole new emphasis into Central America? Are you excited about that added dimension to your work?" She said,

> I can't say I'm excited. I'm trying to learn what I can and then I need to hand off this endeavor to someone with the passion to go at this wholeheartedly. My passion is for kids *here*. It's not that I don't care about kids in other places, but my heart can only take on so much.

After some further interaction, Wendy confessed she has a hard time with Hispanic men. In a previous job, she was repeatedly harassed by a Mexican-American colleague, although she never filed a formal complaint against him. She knew it was unfair to generalize her experience to all Central American men, but she couldn't change the raw emotions she felt about thrusting herself into an environment filled with men who remind her of this past experience.

Despite Wendy's hard work to shore up her Spanish and understanding of Latin culture, her reticence for this cross-cultural project will impede her effectiveness. Most approaches to cross-cultural work focus on information about how cultures differ. But many of the greatest challenges in cross-cultural leadership have much less to do with inadequate information and far more to do with motivation. Without adequate drive and confidence, leaders will continue to struggle in cross-cultural work.

The first step toward leading with cultural intelligence is addressing the motivational issues for ourselves and others. We *can* increase our CQ drive. Researchers Linn Van Dyne and Soon Ang describe three subdimensions of CQ drive: intrinsic motivation, extrinsic motivation, and self-efficacy.[1] Their work strongly informs the following strategies for growing in CQ drive: honesty, self-confidence, eating and socializing, counting the perks, and the triple bottom line.

HOW TO DEVELOP CQ DRIVE

Be honest with yourself.

Examine your confidence level.

Eat and socialize.

Count the perks.

Work for the triple bottom line (fiscal, humanitarian, and environmental).

Key question: What's my level of confidence and motivation for this cross-cultural assignment? If it's lacking, what can I do to increase it?

Be Honest with Yourself

The first important way to enhance CQ drive is to be honest with ourselves. As I questioned Wendy about her upcoming trip, she was able to honestly acknowledge her reservations about immersing herself in the Latin American culture. That's a significant breakthrough.

Some of us love trying new foods. Others hope to sneak aside to eat a taste from home when traveling abroad. Even though I come to life when I'm immersed in a new place, I regularly have my own share of moments when I hit the wall. They don't have to be all-out meltdowns, and they usually aren't. For example, here is a journal entry I wrote when teaching a group of leaders in Malaysia:

> I'm jet-lagged, Em is sick at home, and my teaching didn't go well yesterday. I wish I could jump on a plane and go home. I should know better than to think I can get good responses by asking questions to the whole group, but I didn't want to use smaller discussion groups yesterday. I need a different approach today.

Honestly assessing our level of interest in a cross-cultural assignment is an integral part of becoming more culturally intelligent. For me, the lack of motivation stemmed from wanting to be home with my sick daughter, feeling tired, and questioning my effectiveness. For Wendy, the lack of motivation was rooted in fear.

A similar kind of honesty was needed by Klaus, a German expatriate on a two-year assignment in Nairobi, Kenya. He described the fear his family experienced when they moved to Nairobi from Munich.

> We found ourselves distrusting everyone. We're not by nature like that. But we heard so many stories about expat families being robbed and taken advantage of. My wife resisted hiring domestic help for the longest time for fear of having Kenyans in our home. Eventually we became more relaxed. But the fear factor was a huge challenge for us during our first six months.

Surely it's appropriate to tend to the safety of our families and to find out if and when we're clearly subjecting ourselves to danger. But when we discover our fears are unfounded, as Klaus did, the challenge becomes facing our fears and persevering.

Honesty also requires facing the prejudices and biases we implicitly associate with certain groups of people. Notice the frank, raw musings written by Sharise, a business leader in Portland, Oregon.

Am I a racist? Yesterday when I stopped to get my blood drawn, a black man walked in. I just assumed he was the lab tech. Only later did it become evident he's a physician. . . . Why did I so quickly assume he must be the lab tech? If he had been a white guy, I probably would have guessed he was a doctor.

We all have biases. The key is whether we act upon them. Implicit association tests are tools created to demonstrate how bias affects the way we interact with people. These tests expose the implicit biases we have toward people's skin color, weight, age, and religion. They're fascinating! You can review some of the actual tests by visiting the website http://implicit.harvard.edu/implicit. They're a great tool to demonstrate the automatic impulses we have toward certain cultural groups. The goal is to be honest about our biases instead of pretending they don't exist. Although our internal biases are automatic, honestly understanding them can help to control and moderate our interactions. We can make a deliberate choice to suspend any judgments that we're biased to make.

A great way to begin developing CQ drive is through being honest with ourselves. It might simply be honestly admitting that you don't particularly enjoy cross-cultural interactions and experiences. Owning that sentiment is a great start. Then we can begin to look at how to connect things that *do* motivate us with our cross-cultural work. Write it down, talk with a trusted friend, and verbalize what energizes you about your cross-cultural work and what leaves you fatigued, fearful, or just unmotivated. Honesty itself is not enough to motivate us, but CQ drive begins with honestly assessing our level of interest in cross-cultural work.

Examine Your Confidence Level

Being honest with ourselves naturally moves us toward the next important way to grow CQ drive—examining our level of confidence for doing cross-cultural work. Self-efficacy is the perception we have of our ability to reach a goal. It's our confidence regarding whether we can succeed at a particular task. A great deal of research supports the premise that a leader's level of confidence in accomplishing what he or she sets out to do will critically determine the outcome.[2]

Wendy demonstrated a great deal of self-efficacy as she described the broader goals for her organization. The budget was 300 percent larger than when she came five years ago and they were helping five times as many children. And she was pretty certain they would continue on that kind of growth curve for the next five years. But the expansion into Central America felt disorienting to Wendy. Her prior experiences eroded her confidence for working there.

Self-efficacy is an important predictor of cross-cultural adjustment.[3] Without a strong sense of self-efficacy, a leader will avoid challenges and give up easily when confronted with setbacks.[4] Wendy tried to build her confidence by learning everything she could about the culture and the children at risk throughout the region. This is certainly a helpful strategy.[5] Wendy's challenge was to tap into this growing understanding to increase her self-confidence for working in Central America. We're more likely to be successful in cross-cultural contexts when we believe we'll be successful at it.

For me, looking at my low motivation and confidence for teaching in Malaysia caused me to spontaneously shift my topic for the day. We were supposed to continue a subject we began the day before—coaching and mentoring. I knew I could cover the material, but I lacked confidence I could get the participants engaged in discussing it beyond what we had done on the previous day. I had recently been thinking a lot about organizational culture and a number of my informal conversations with these seminar participants were related to issues going on within their various organizations. So I shifted to this topic because I felt more confident about doing it with them. We used a number of group exercises where I assigned them various organizational cultures and suggested some concrete ways for them to use the insights they had discovered. I had to deal with some dissonance this created for some participants who wanted to make sure we were going to finish covering the coaching and mentoring material promised—a fair concern by any group and accentuated by the cultural values of some of the participants. But the room felt like it had come alive. It may have been the content and topic, but it just as well might have been the shift in my personal sense of confidence that this would be something that would better connect. Our sense of confidence for particular tasks varies based on the situation and context. Growing our confidence will enhance our CQ drive.

Eat and Socialize

In addition to honesty and self-confidence, a far more concrete motivational issue is eating and hanging out with people. Food is one of the most familiar topics discussed among international travelers. Many business travelers describe the challenge of eating unfamiliar foods and the "scary" experience of being hosted by people who appear insensitive to a visitor's dislike for the local cuisine. Aini, an Indonesian executive, talked with me about the challenges she felt during her first business trip to the United States. She said,

> I still haven't acquired a taste for all the raw greens you Americans love. Your salads are huge but they're pretty uninviting to me. And having seen the way they package up chicken and freeze it, I can't bring myself to eat the cold chicken often put in the salad. It can't be fresh like the whole ones we get at the markets in Jakarta. When I buy chicken or fish at home, I can see what it looks like before it gets all diced up. But it just turns my stomach to walk through the meat section in the supermarkets in the United States. I just dread mealtime when I'm in the States.

It's ironic to hear Aini describe her distaste for frozen chicken in similar ways to how many Americans describe the nauseating experience of seeing fresh meat hanging in local markets in Asia. Aini's disgust for American food isn't likely to be as detrimental to her when working in the United States as it would be in some other places. For the most part, food plays a very functional role in American culture. We eat to work. If Aini was visiting in my home, I'd tell her, "Don't eat anything you don't like. We don't care." And we really wouldn't for the most part. But in many parts of the world, food is deeply rooted in the life of people. Sometimes I've had Indian hosts prepare meals for me that used spices grown on their homestead for hundreds of years. The best Indian meals take days to prepare. So to pass on eating dishes prepared for you in that context could be far more insulting than passing on a dish you just don't care for. It can be seen as an all-out rejection. And as for eating with utensils versus eating with our hands, one of my Indian friends puts it this way: "Eating with utensils is like making love through an interpreter!" That says it all when it comes to the affection most Indians have for their cuisine. To reject the food of an Indian colleague can be extremely disrespectful and can erode any possibility of a business partnership. Who would have thought food could play such a strong role in successful global performance?

Edwin, a British executive from a Fortune 500 company who often travels to Southeast Asia, observed the huge advantage his love for trying new foods played in his negotiation strategies. Edwin made this observation when reflecting on his regular travels to Southeast Asia:

My hosts are often keen to bring me to places with Western food. They're amazed when I tell them I really want the local food instead. Again and again, they tell me how unusual it is for them to have a Western guest as adventurous as me. Spicy noodles, exotic seafood, fish eyes, frog, snake, insects — I've tried a lot of interesting things. . . . It's at these extended dinner meetings after a long day in the office that the real business transactions happen. I'm convinced this is one of the most important strategies for international business.

Edwin also insisted that most of the contracts he has negotiated in Southeast Asia happened over shared meals together, not during the formal business meetings during the day. You don't have to be as adventurous as Edwin to gain some of the value that comes from trying new foods. Making an honest attempt to try something goes a long way. For those who grow queasy thinking about it, here are some strategies you might consider:

* Always try at least a few bites.
* Don't ask what it is. Sometimes the idea makes it seem worse than it actually tastes. Just eat it, with obvious exceptions for food allergies.
* Slice it thin and swallow quickly.
* If the texture bothers you, add good amounts of rice, noodles, or bread to provide a firmer texture to squishy foods.
* Pineapple tempers the bite of hot, spicy foods and Coca-Cola makes it burn more. Eat and drink accordingly.
* If you aren't sure *how* to eat it (e.g., with your hands, what to peel off), just ask. Most hosts will love showing you.
* Find something about the food you can compliment and do everything you can to avoid a negative facial expression. You *are* being watched!
* Ask your host about any significance the dish might have to them personally or in the culture.
* Beware. You might actually find some things you start craving when you get home!

In most cultures, eating together has far more symbolic value than simply "grabbing a bite to eat." Sharing a meal together can often be viewed as a sacred event. The same can be true in many places when we're invited to do some sightseeing. An American executive visiting a branch office in Thailand might feel like a ride down the Chao Phraya River in a river taxi is a waste of time. And a German executive might feel that eating the local food with Kenyan bureaucrats has little influence on getting a factory built. However, research demonstrates exactly the opposite. Our level of interest in connecting with the culture and the people as a whole will directly shape how well we do our work in subtle but profound ways. Furthermore, while sightseeing might seem like a waste of time for those from more industrialized, developed countries, it demonstrates respect for the history and traditions of a culture and its people and it helps in developing relationships with colleagues in another context. The importance of this is usually missed by those of us coming from cultures with less emphasis on history.

One of the challenges I've discovered with all this eating and socializing is that cultural differences are more pronounced in social settings than in work settings. For example, a software developer can often talk in "code" with another software developer and immediately find some common ground. The same is true between a Brazilian and German sociologist or a Chinese and Canadian CEO. Without question, there are challenges and differences in a cross-cultural work setting, but on the whole we can relate more easily with our professional counterparts when talking shop than when we venture into the social context. Many of our work environments have some cultural norms that offer needed cues for how to behave. However, many of these norms are absent once we move into a social setting. Many of the greatest cross-cultural challenges experienced by foreigners occur over dinner after work.

As a result, the energy required to socially interact with people from different cultural backgrounds often causes us to retreat to more familiar and comfortable social contexts. Short-term business travelers usually feel more comfortable when traveling with other colleagues from home and eating familiar food. Executives fulfilling an expatriate assignment often cloister themselves in the expat subculture rather than immerse themselves locally. However, we're much less likely to succeed in a cross-cultural setting when we withdraw from it or remain with a large group of colleagues from home. When we come into a new environment together as a group of outsiders, we have a built-in support group and point of identification. As a result, we aren't as motivated to integrate ourselves into the local setting.[6]

We need to relate this CQ drive practice — eating and socializing — with the first one we discussed, which was being honest with ourselves. Introverts, in particular, will quickly be drained by all the hard work of socializing cross-culturally. And all of us will find occasions, especially when immersed in ongoing, extended work cross-culturally, when we need to withdraw for a while, either to spend time with people from a familiar cultural context or to have time alone with some of the comforts of home. I think any business traveler can survive for a few days without McDonald's and Starbucks. But there's a time when tapping into the comforts of home can help to sustain the ongoing CQ drive needed. There's nothing wrong with retreating from time to time to recharge our batteries. But if we aren't careful, we'll find ourselves progressively drawn away from the local culture. What was meant to be a time of recharging will come at the expense of engaging with the local culture.[7] When we look for familiar foods and crave a current copy of *USA Today* on our way to a negotiation meeting, we may as a result miss out on a huge leveraging opportunity. Think twice before eating at McDonald's and skipping the dinner invitation.

Count the Perks

The fatigue, fears, and anxieties that accompany cross-cultural work can be overwhelming, but be encouraged that there are some rewarding payoffs. I'm not just talking about frequent flyer miles and souvenirs for the family. There are some tangible benefits for leaders who learn how to successfully adapt to different cultures. Stepping back to consider the benefits is an important way to motivate yourself and others to continually develop cultural intelligence. Here are a few of the perks that result from persevering through the challenges and opportunities of cross-cultural leadership:

- *Career Advancement.* Growing numbers of healthy organizations require that anyone becoming a senior leader must first be proven in working with a multicultural team. Several corporations now require at least two different international assignments in difficult locations before an individual will be considered for an executive-level role. Jack Welch, the former head of General Electric, has said: "The Jack Welch of the future cannot be like me. I've spent my entire career in the United States. The next head of GE will be someone who has spent time in Bombay, in Hong Kong, and in Buenos Aires."[8]
- *Creativity and Innovation.* Learning to negotiate and expand internationally fosters a sense of creativity that can't be gained any other way. The art of negotiation is challenging enough when cultures are shared. But learning how to reach a win-win outcome when dealing with multiple cultural backgrounds grows an overall sense of innovation and creativity that can be applied across many other facets of life and work. It's one thing to understand the cultural differences between German and Chinese cultures. It's quite another thing to have creatively found a way to develop a working relationship that achieves the respective performance objectives while also demonstrating dignity and honor for one another.
- *Expansion of Global Networks.* Social networking is the buzz these days. And interacting with people from various cultural backgrounds, both at home and around the world, can be

personally enriching and can open up all kinds of additional opportunities. Note the personal and professional opportunities that exist from connecting with individuals from a vast array of backgrounds and networks by going outside your familiar context and into new ones.

- *Salary and Profit.* Given the 70 percent failure rate of all international ventures, many organizations are willing to pay for talent that can successfully perform in intercultural situations because doing so yields higher profits. It doesn't take long to see the benefit to the organization as well as to the individual when calculating the cost of a leader who is *ineffective* working across cultures. Consider the following:
  - Which senior-level leaders have had to deal with the fallout from an unsuccessful cross-cultural venture? What's their pay? Try putting an hourly rate on their time. How many hours have been spent by senior leaders dealing with this situation? Just a few meetings a week put you into hundreds of hours multiplied by these leaders' hourly rates.
  - Add the cost of other staff who get engaged in it.
  - Then add the cost of missed opportunities because of all the energy diverted toward this issue.
  - Then imagine the cost of what this does to the overall morale and future growth of the organization.

You get the idea. However, if we aren't careful, it's easy to see cultural intelligence as a nice lofty ideal and miss its connection to our P&L reports. Prioritizing cultural intelligence across an organization is proven to play a role in increased profit margins.[9] Therefore, increased wages for those who can succeed at international work are well worth the investment.

There are some definite perks that come with cross-cultural work. Rewarding ourselves and team members who do that work well is a helpful way to increase CQ drive.

Work for the Triple Bottom Line

Although extrinsic motivators like advancement in career and salary are valid, at some point culturally intelligent leaders need to consider something bigger as the ongoing source of motivation for culturally intelligent behavior. At the end of the day, a bigger cause is needed to sustain CQ drive.

Peter Wege, retired chairman of office furniture maker Steelcase, popularized the term *triple bottom line,* meaning businesses need to be equally responsible for fiscal profit, human welfare, and environmental responsibility. He argues that all three areas are the measure of today's successful business.[10] A growing movement of top-level executives are asking: What goes along with the profits being made? How does our work affect the environment? Are we causing people suffering, despair, or injustice in the process of making a profit?

At some level, every organization needs to be fiscally profitable. Even nonprofit organizations can't meet the needs of their "customers" without economic viability. And without a profit, an organization can't continue to exist. Ironically, the other two bottom lines—environmental responsibility and human welfare—need not conflict with fiscal gain. All three areas can serve each other. There may be times to give up a profit-producing opportunity because it violates the other two bottom lines. However, the emphasis here is more about how we perform and how we use the money made. Money can be used to offer people opportunity, life sustenance, and empowerment or it can be used to destroy life.[11]

The three bottom lines are indispensible to one another as we tap into a globalized market and workforce. Many companies across the world today realize success requires earning the respect and confidence of their customers. It's no longer a matter of simply adhering to legal rules and regulations. Whether it's safety standards, child labor practices, or discrimination in hiring, customers are regulating how we do our work.

A deeper, altruistic drive is a far more sustainable motivation for CQ than merely pursuing global markets for selfish interests. In fact, cultural intelligence cannot exist apart from true love for the world and for people.[12] At the very core of cultural intelligence is the desire to learn with and about other people. So we must beware of penetrating the cultural contexts of other groups and imposing our views of life on them. Instead, our global operations give us a chance to gain mutually beneficial insights and beliefs from trans-continental relationships.

What might a more transcendent motivation look like for those readers from the United States? Perhaps a specific word of caution is needed for us. For several years, there was a sense that a leader from the United States could be welcomed anywhere in the world with our services, products, and ideas. But in recent years, there's been a sea change of attitudes toward the United States and what it means to work with us. International leaders in business, government, and nonprofit organizations whisper behind closed doors about the way visiting Americans live in their own bubbles without having much genuine interaction with their overseas counterparts, much less the locals. One senior foreign policy advisor told Fareed Zakaria of *Newsweek*, "When we meet with American officials, they talk and we listen—we rarely disagree or speak frankly because they simply can't take it in."[13] Kishore Mahbubani, Singapore's former foreign secretary and ambassador to the United Nations, put it this way: "There are two sets of conversations, one with Americans in the room and one without."[14] We've come by this reputation naturally by having dominated the world on so many fronts for the last century. But as emerging markets continue to rise, particularly in China, India, Russia, and Brazil, we have to change our role from superpower to more of a global broker. As we posture ourselves with a spirit of openness, collaboration, and even compromise, we may regain a reputation for being a nation known for innovation, and as Zakaria says, "a place where people from all over the world can work, mingle, mix, and share in a common dream and a common destiny."[15] American leaders need not perpetuate the ugly American syndrome nor do we have to give up playing a significant role in global affairs. But we need to reshape our perspective on what we have to offer and gain from international markets.

On the other hand, while some leaders from emerging economies might secretly revel in the marginalization of Western influence, caution is appropriate for them as well. Instead, these leaders ought to consider how to use their growing influence and power to help other developing nations have a place at the table, too. Leaders from places like China and Saudi Arabia can readily identify with what it's like to be the underdog and they can draw on that understanding to increase their altruistic drive to help others. They might even consider the counterintuitive move of coming alongside leaders in places like Japan, Germany, and the United States to help them reinvent themselves in this new era of globalization. These are far more compelling reasons for cross-cultural effectiveness than merely pursuing self-interests.

The call toward something bigger can play a powerful role in increasing our overall CQ drive. In fact, perhaps the greatest way for Wendy to enhance her self-efficacy and CQ drive for her upcoming trip and future work in Central America is by tapping into her humanitarian orientation. As CEO of an organization committed to underprivileged children, she cares deeply about the pursuit of fairness and equity for all children. Tapping into her altruistic motivation to help children might be what she needs most to compel her to persevere despite some of the cultural dissonance she anticipates and will likely face. The same is true for Klaus, the German expatriate in Nairobi. When he no longer views Kenyans as merely the people to use to help his company get ahead, it can help mitigate some of the fears he and his family feel about living in Kenya. As he begins to enjoy the opportunity and wonder of working and relating with Kenyan people, he'll tap into a life-giving discovery.

CQ drive rests in something bigger than us. The challenge for us as leaders is to see our existence not only in terms of our own interests but ultimately about things larger than us. If more power, wealth, and success are all that drive us, we'll face burnout pretty fast. But as we and our organizations use the triple bottom line to fit into things larger than us, join them, and serve them, we can take our role in the big picture and find ourselves with heightened energy for persevering through the hard work of cross-cultural leadership. Life is about things that transcend us.[16]

Conclusion

CQ drive goes beyond the excitement of traveling to a new place. It's the perseverance required when the novelty wears off and the differences start to chafe at us. We have to move beyond our fear, be willing to take risks, and grow in our ability to perform effectively in places that seem more foreign than familiar. Trying new foods, taking in some of the local culture, and persevering through the fatigue of relating cross-culturally offers great benefits.

Work teams often have a high level of motivation to successfully accomplish a specific task. Software programmers working with virtual colleagues across multiple locations want to meet deadlines. Designers want to be sure their manufacturing colleagues create the product originally envisioned. Doctors and nurses want to correctly diagnose what's ailing an immigrant. Accounting firms want to see accuracy across the spreadsheets analyzed by a multicultural team of personnel. If that kind of successful performance is what motivates you most, use that motivation to help you persevere through eating unfamiliar foods, straining to know what to talk about, and learning how to take on the perspective of the people you encounter. That will all be part of increasing your effectiveness. Although the work of CQ drive is never really done, at some level, it becomes more familiar and comfortable the more we do it. I don't know that it ever becomes easy but the benefits of persevering through these challenges are immense, in terms of both how it allows you to accomplish your work-related objectives and the portal it gives you to see the world through different eyes.

CQ drive is the first step toward gaining the benefits from cultural intelligence. We can begin by honestly facing our fears, biases, and level of confidence. And remember that Big Mac or salad you're craving in Shanghai could cost you the contract! But by trying the fish eyes served, you could win friends, secure a big account, and move us one step closer to making the world a better place.

BEST PRACTICES FOR CQ DRIVE

1. *Calculate the personal, organizational, and global cost of not prioritizing cultural intelligence.* An honest assessment can quickly motivate you and your team to grow your CQ.

2. *Connect your cross-cultural assignment with other interests.* If you aren't naturally motivated to experience different cultures, find a way to connect the assignment with something that does interest you. If you like art, what artistic expressions can you discover? If you love sports, discover what sports are hot there. If you're a foodie, the options are endless. If you eat, drink, and sleep business, use this as a way to learn new business insights.

3. *Accept whatever cross-cultural assignments are available.* Direct experience working in cross-cultural situations, watching others who do it successfully, and learning "on the job" is one of the most important ways to gain confidence to do it more. Multiple international experiences, work and nonwork, are among the best ways to develop CQ drive.[17]

4. *Try the local specialties.* Most places around the world are gaining more ethnic diversity in the foods available. Break out of your routine and try new foods. And especially when

visiting another place, always try at least a few bites. Slice it thin and swallow quickly if you must. But eat, eat, eat!

5. *Live for something bigger.* We were made for more than working ourselves to death and making money. Some of us may take on causes on a large scale. Others of us will mentor one business leader and make his or her life better. Cultural intelligence offers a way of making the world a better place.

CHAPTER 4

STUDY THE TOPOGRAPHY: CQ KNOWLEDGE
(STEP 2A)

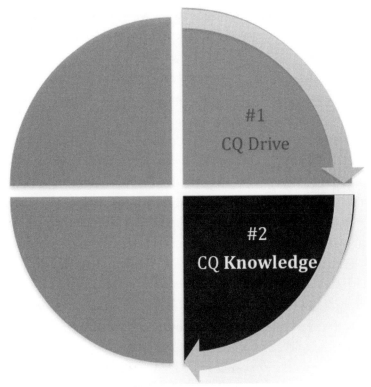

STEP 2: CQ KNOWLEDGE: What do I need to know?	
Understanding cross-cultural issues and differences	
Profile of a leader with high CQ knowledge:	Leaders high in CQ knowledge have a rich, well-organized understanding of culture and how it affects the way people think and behave. They possess a repertoire of knowledge in knowing how cultures are alike and different. They understand how culture shapes behavior.

"**C**an we *please* eat something *normal* tonight?!" It's the kind of question I'm pretty used to hearing, after having spent several years working in and out of a lot of different cultural contexts. But this time, the question was coming from my own daughter! My family was along with me for a three-week work trip in Southeast Asia. Although Western food was readily available in most of the places we traveled, my wife and I were soaking up the chance to eat some great Asian food. Looking straight into her brilliant blue eyes I quickly retorted, "Emily. You want something *normal?*" (insert lots of emphasis and sarcasm on the word *normal*). "You can't get much more *normal* than rice. Do you know how many people eat rice in the world? That's about as *normal* as you can get." Before I could go any further, my wife gave me the *look*. You know the kind. She didn't have to say a word. I knew it meant something like, *Save your cross-cultural lecture for later. Let's just buy them a burger and fries.* Two minutes later we were standing in line at Burger King. Not to fear, in this case, it didn't cost me a contract with a client.

Ethnocentrism—evaluating other people and their culture by the standards of our own cultural preferences—is found among people everywhere. Seeing the world in light of our own cultural background and experience is inevitable. However, ignoring the impact of ethnocentrism on how we lead is the single greatest obstacle to CQ knowledge. Most of us tend to underestimate the degree to which we ourselves are a product of culture. It's much easier to see it in others. Emily's question made explicit a guiding assumption for many of us: *My experience is what's normal and best.* Nowadays, Emily is as quick to catch me in my cultural blind spots as I am her. The other day we were driving by a fluorescent green house in a neighborhood otherwise filled with earth tone–colored homes. "Now that's just weird!" I blurted out. Emily chimed in, "Dad, don't you mean 'different'?" Touché! I tend to be more sensitive and respectful of differences in faraway places than I do when I encounter them closer to home. Is it really such a big deal to think neon-colored homes and unfamiliar foods are "abnormal" or weird? Maybe and maybe not. But to remain unaware of how culture shapes the way people think and behave is not only foolish, it's expensive. From Wal-Mart-size businesses to mom-and-pop shops around the world, research consistently demonstrates a high level of failure when expansion into international markets is done without an awareness of how people from other cultures think and behave.

After eight years of struggling in Germany, Wal-Mart sold its eighty-five stores there. Many journalists have theorized about what led to Wal-Mart's failure given the company's wild success at home, but it's widely agreed that Wal-Mart's primary flaw was in ignoring the cultural differences between the United States and Germany. The company tried to apply its U.S. success formula to a German market without modifying it. Whether it was the kinds of products offered, the way in which items were displayed, or the policies used in the employee handbook, Wal-Mart's stint in Germany seems to be a case study of what happens when greater attention isn't given to the powerful role of culture. As a result, Wal-Mart filed a loss of USD $1 billion.[1]

Even if an organization never expands internationally, it's impossible to be an effective leader without some insight into how culture shapes the thoughts and behavior of the people touched by your leadership. In fact, Edgar Schein, author of the best-selling book *Organizational Culture and Leadership,* says it's impossible to separate culture and leadership. Schein says that cultural norms significantly influence how you define leadership—for example, who should get promoted, what success is, and how to motivate employees. He argues that *creating and managing culture* is the only thing of real importance for leaders. Schein writes, "The unique talent of leaders is their ability to understand and work with culture"—both the organizational and the socioethnic cultures they regularly encounter.[2] Don't dismiss cultural understanding as a politically correct, touchy-feely topic. It will define your leadership.

The ability to understand and work with culture does not just come intuitively. It requires a disciplined effort to grow in the competency of cultural understanding, or CQ knowledge. CQ knowledge, or step two in the cycle toward cultural intelligence, refers to our level of understanding about a culture and the ways cultures differ. In this chapter and Chapter 5, we'll review the most important cultural knowledge needed by leaders. The subdimensions of CQ knowledge are knowledge about cultural systems, norms, and values.[3] These subdimensions will surface in the strategies we cover for developing CQ knowledge. First, we'll learn how to see culture and its role in the way we think, behave, and lead. Then we'll review the most relevant cultural systems and values that need to be understood. And we'll conclude by seeing the value of understanding different languages. Given the volume of information relevant to CQ knowledge, the material for Step 2 is divided across two chapters. You might breeze through this information now and later refer to it more deliberately when running through this second step of cultural intelligence in preparation for a particular cross-cultural task. In this chapter, we'll look at the first two ways to develop CQ knowledge: (1) see culture's role in yourself and others, and (2) review the basic cultural systems.

HOW TO DEVELOP CQ KNOWLEDGE

See culture's role in yourself and others.

Review the basic cultural systems.

Learn the core cultural values.

Understand different languages.

Key question: What cultural understanding do I need for this cross-cultural assignment?

See Culture's Role in Yourself and Others

A way to begin growing CQ knowledge is to see the way culture shapes what we see, how we think, and what we do. This means understanding the cultural center of ourselves and others. Our cultural center is the inner core that shapes the way we live and make sense of the world. This understanding begins by making the notion of culture more explicit.

One time my friend Vijay took me to a cricket match in Delhi. I went because I wanted to hang out with Vijay, not because I really wanted to watch cricket. I had tried watching a few matches on TV before, but I always found myself entirely lost. Vijay was a great teacher, though. As we watched the game in the sweltering heat, he started to explain the basic rules, the use of the wickets, the way scoring happened, and the ultimate goal of getting each batsman on the opponent's team out. Not only was the game starting to make sense but I actually felt myself getting drawn into the excitement of the competition. It would have been a sorry sight if I had actually tried to get out on the field and play. But at least I grew in my understanding of what was going on while the cricket professionals played their game.

CQ knowledge provides a similar kind of understanding and perspective for the cultures with which we interact as leaders. It involves understanding the rules, albeit often unspoken ones, that are behind the behavior occurring within a particular culture — whether among an ethnic group, an organizational culture, or the subculture of a political party or religious group. The objective of the acquired understanding isn't to become like the people in that cultural group or to be able to play their games. The goal is to understand and appreciate the rules behind their lives and society. CQ knowledge begins with simply understanding the powerful role of culture in ourselves and others.

Basically, the term *culture* is a way of describing how and why people do what they do. Cricket players and enthusiasts don't consciously think about all the rules and rationale behind the game while they're in the midst of it, but those rules shape everything going on. In the same way, culture consists of the rules and rationale behind the way life gets played in a particular context.

The most familiar way of thinking about a cultural group is as a national culture — the norms, customs, and values shared with people who live in a country. For example, Switzerland has a national culture even though the country includes a variety of regions, each with its own languages and ethnic traditions. There's an overarching way of seeing the world that's common to most Swiss people. Understanding differences between one national culture and another is a good starting point for CQ knowledge. Although many subcultures exist within most countries, national culture is the cultural orientation that most significantly shapes how most people think and behave.

The other culture most consistently encountered by leaders is organizational culture. Organizations and even professions have their own distinct values, norms, and ways of viewing people and issues. Businesses have distinct ways of celebrating successes, motivating employees, and telling their stories. The same is true of universities, hospitals, and temples. And there are endless other subcultures we encounter day in and day out, including cultures organized around generational differences, sexual orientation, professional guilds, hobbies, regions within a country, religions, and many more. Each of us is a member of numerous different cultural contexts, as are the people we lead.

We aren't merely passive recipients of culture in any of these contexts. Culture isn't something that just happens to us; rather we're also active creators of it. Many leaders inherit organizational cultures with unhealthy practices and dysfunctional behavior throughout the company. It's extremely challenging to change an organizational culture, but it can be done. And we play a role in morphing and adapting the national cultures of which we are a part.[4]

Leaders, more than anyone else in an organization, need to be conscious of how culture shapes the behavior of themselves and others. Wendy, the CEO of the children-at-risk organization mentioned earlier, is a great picture of a leader who is very aware of culture's influence on the way she works. Despite the motivational challenges she faced with expanding into Central America, she showed me a list of questions she was trying to get answered to think about her strategy for Central America. In addition, she talked about the differences between the programs her organization used in New York compared with those in Los Angeles. Most of her board members are corporate executives so she presents the budget and strategic plan to them in an entirely different format from what she uses with her personnel and she uses yet another strategy with volunteers and donors. Wendy represents a leader who sees the powerful role of culture in how people think and behave.

Not everyone, however, is as convinced about the relevance of cultural understanding. Jeff, an American sales representative from a large manufacturing company, participated in one of our studies that examined the perceived value midlevel managers ascribe to cultural intelligence. Jeff is a stocky forty-two-year-old from the central part of the United States. When I interviewed him, he was just a week away from making his second business trip to China to visit a couple of factories in Guangzhou that were manufacturing his product line.

Jeff was very animated as we interacted together. With his legs constantly moving up and down and his fingers nervously tapping on the table, he said, "Okay, no offense man. But doesn't this whole cultural thing get a little overplayed? I mean, people are people and business is business. I'll probably have to eat some weird food next week, but otherwise, I don't see what the big differences are."

I resisted jumping in for the moment and I listened as Jeff carried on with his line of reasoning. Continuing with his rapid rate of speech, Jeff said,

The way I see it, everyone is just trying to find a way to make a decent living and get ahead in life. I don't care whether you're Chinese, Mexican, or American, people are pretty much the same. They care about their kids like you and me. They know you have to be aggressive to survive in this global market. And everyone wants to make a decent living. The marketing strategy might need to adapt a little bit but I think manufacturing is manufacturing and selling is selling, wherever you go. Either you're cut out for it or not!

There's certainly some merit to what Jeff is saying. There are some universal characteristics we share with everyone. A leader's ability to distinguish between what's universal, what's cultural, and what's personal is one of the most important indicators of cultural intelligence. This discernment stems from basic CQ knowledge. The iceberg is a metaphor I often use to talk about this idea. (See Figure 4-1.) The tip of the iceberg, visible above sea level, includes things universally shared by all humanity. But when you begin to go deeper, you find there are a slew of differences attributable to varying cultures and individual personalities. This is an important point of understanding. We'll refer back to these three categories of human behavior (universal, cultural, and personal norms) many more times in the book.

Universal

Jeff's statement "people are people" has a measure of truth. There are things we share with almost every human being. I love to sit in a busy train station or mall and watch all the people. Even in a faraway place where I don't know anyone, I can feel a level of connection simply by watching a dad with his kids, a fellow traveler with her bags, or a couple laughing together. We all have common fears. We all have some basic needs that have to get met. And almost all parents care about their kids. It's appropriate to acknowledge the human

Figure 4-1.   Three Categories of Human Behavior

UNIVERSAL

CULTURAL

Cultural Artifacts and Systems
art, clothing, food, money, customs, gestures, etc.

Cultural Values and Assumptions
Unconscious, taken-for-granted beliefs, percep-tions, and feelings

PERSONAL

characteristics shared by most everyone. These are the universals with which we begin our understanding as we relate and lead.

Cultural

When I move beyond feeling a connection with a stranger interact-ing with his child to making assumptions about their relationship based on my observations alone, I move into questionable terri-tory. Or if I had made judgments about the cricket game I watched based on the rules of football, I'd have surely misinterpreted what was going on.

As noted in Figure 4-1, some of what makes up a culture is vis-ible. The way people drive, the local currency, religious symbols, or the way a business images itself are things that can be observed and identified. These are the visible cues about cultural differences that exist in a society. But the most important points of understand-ing are the thoughts, values, and assumptions that lie beneath the surface of what's visible. As represented by the iceberg, beneath the surface of a culture are the beliefs, values, and assumptions that drive behavior.

If Jeff fails to see the profound differences that exist between the way a Chinese business partner thinks and behaves as compared with an American one, he's sure to hit all kinds of roadblocks. And ignorance about the cultural differences that abound in the multicultural workforce around us puts us on the pathway toward ineffective, irrelevant leadership.

Let's just consider the Chinese concept of *guanxi* to think about why cultural difference is something Jeff needs to bear in mind. *Guanxi* refers to the connections and resulting obligations that exist between two individuals. It exists between Chinese families first and foremost, but it's also found among classmates and professional colleagues because of their shared history. It results in individuals loosely keeping track of the favors given and the debts owed between one another. Given the underlying presence of *guanxi* in most Chinese relationships, Jeff would be wise to learn the significance of the gifts he may be given by his colleagues in Guangzhou as a way to establish and build a relationship together. The same actions done at home might appear to be bribery or little more than just a token gesture. But misunderstanding what this means in China could derail everything Jeff has been sent there to do.

Culture *does* matter and shapes how we ought to do our work. A former U.S. ambassador to Yemen and the United Arab Emirates describes a career of having watched a continual stream of U.S. salespeople moving in and out of the Persian Gulf to sell their goods and services. All too often, he saw U.S. sales reps losing opportunities to their British, French, or Japanese counterparts because they tried to use the same sales pitch from home in the Middle East. Meanwhile, he observed many businesspeople from other countries spent more time learning about the local culture and even the local language and, as a result, secured contracts lost by their U.S. counterparts.[5]

Culture is everywhere. It's shaping what you're thinking and seeing right now. And it shapes the way *you* are being viewed by people from other cultural contexts. There will be assumptions made about Jeff, accurate or inaccurate, simply because he's a U.S. businessman. A recent study asked people in a variety of places around the world to share their two predominant images of the United States. The winners were war and the TV show *Baywatch!*[6] In a post-9/11 era, it takes little guessing to figure out why many people in the world equate the United States with war. As for *Baywatch*, it's the most exported U.S. television program in the world.[7]

Jeff might be an American pacifist who has no clue who David Hasselhoff is. But that doesn't change the fact that when many people in the world see Jeff with a U.S. passport, they'll automatically form assumptions about him that might involve images of war and *Baywatch*. I'm an American, married white guy with a Ph.D. who lives and works in the Midwest. Talk about an identity loaded with preconceived notions by people. Part of my learning how to adeptly interact with people from various cultural contexts is having some sense of how they may perceive me simply because of the cultural groups of which I'm a part. CQ knowledge begins with an understanding of how culture shapes us, others, and the perceptions we have of one another. Culture is everywhere and it influences what's going on. Can you see it?

Personal

At the deepest level of the iceberg are our individual differences. Leaders functioning at the highest levels of cultural intelligence are able to see when the behavior of others is a reflection of their cultural background and when it's idiosyncratic behavior. There are things I do that are stereotypical of how most Americans behave. And there are characteristics of me that would be unfair to generalize to all Americans. A culturally intelligent leader will learn to identify the personal quirks and characteristics of individuals versus those that fit cultural norms.

Describing personal preferences and behaviors as cultural behavior is one of the most consistent errors made by people during cross-cultural interactions. One Canadian manager told me she had a Sikh Indian man working for her. She said, "One of the things I've noticed about Sikhs is they don't like to travel. Every time I ask Mr. Singh to attend a meeting out of town, he comes up with an excuse." When I asked her whether she had observed this among other Sikh employees, she said that Mr. Singh was actually the only Sikh she knew personally. But she just assumed it was a cultural thing because who wouldn't want to get out of London, Ontario, every once in a while at the company's expense? She presumed any unfamiliar, inexplicable behavior she observed in him must be due to his cultural background. This works the other way, too. There might be a cultural norm that tends to be true of most Sikhs, such as "Most Sikhs are deeply spiritual people." It would be appropriate to consider whether that norm applies to Mr. Singh. But just as this manager can't presume everything about Mr. Singh applies to all Sikhs, so also she can't assume that everything about Sikhs applies to Mr. Singh.

Later, we'll note the value of using cultural norms and values as a starting point for understanding others. But caution is always needed. Cultural intelligence is required to discern among what's universal, what's cultural, and what's personal. The rest of the material on CQ knowledge highlights issues related to the middle layer of the iceberg—understanding cultural systems, values, and language.

Review the Basic Cultural Systems

The first way to see beyond our universal similarities is to understand the varying ways cultures address the common needs shared by all humans, which are cultural systems. Without careful observation, the significance of these systems can be easily missed.

We're going to examine the following cultural systems: economic, marriage and family, educational, legal and political, religious, and artistic.

Economic Systems: Capitalist vs. Socialist

Every society has to come up with some basic ways of meeting its members' universal needs of food, water, clothing, and housing. Understanding how a society has organized itself to produce, allocate, and distribute these basic resources is extremely important to culturally intelligent leadership. Most of us are pretty familiar with the two most predominant economic systems today: capitalism and socialism. Capitalism, found in countries like the United States, is based on the principle of individuals gaining resources and services according to their capacity to pay for them. The assumption underlying capitalism is that individuals are motivated to care for themselves and the market exists to meet the needs of individuals. Competition is seen as good for the consumer and thus for the whole society. On the other end of the spectrum is socialism, found in countries like China and Cuba. The state plays a much more active role in the production and distribution of basic resources by ensuring some equality of access for everyone in society to basic resources. Most of us have pretty strong feelings about which one of these systems is superior, but we must beware of assuming there is only one right way to distribute goods and services. Most economies today are a mixture of capitalism and socialism and there is a wide range of other possibilities, particularly in more tribal contexts. You don't need to be an expert on how the entire economic system works in every culture; but a general awareness of the differing ways in which economic systems are organized will enhance the ability to negotiate and develop a working relationship outside your own national culture. The summary in Table 4-1 is something you can reference in the future to apply this understanding to your leadership.

Table 4-1.   Economic Systems

Economic Systems
The basic ways a society organizes itself to meet its members' universal needs of food, water, clothing, and housing.

Capitalism:	Socialism:
A society created around the idea of individuals gaining resources and services based on their capacity to pay for them. Decisions are market driven.	A society in which the state coordinates and implements the production and distribution of basic resources through central planning and control.

Leadership Implications:
• Consider how to best motivate personnel in light of the predominant economic system. Competition tends to be a better motivational strategy in capitalist societies and cooperation in socialist ones. • Understand which industries in a particular place are state run and which ones are privatized. And be alert that even some privatized companies have heavy state-level investment. • When expanding your organization into a country with a different economic system, consider what human resource policies will need to be revised in light of the way health care and retirement are done, how to do performance reviews, and appropriate compensation.

Marriage and Family Systems: Kinship vs. Nuclear Family

Each society also has a way for working out a system for who can marry whom, under what conditions, and according to what procedures. A related system of child care becomes standardized in most cultures. The most commonly described family systems are kinship systems versus nuclear family systems. Most of the world is organized around kinship-based societies where blood relationship and solidarity within one's family and clan is central. This is called *consanguine kinship*, where identity rests mostly on how individuals are genealogically connected. Kinship societies are made up of extended families where the household often includes three or more generations.

In contrast, the nuclear-family system, sometimes called *affinial kinship,* is found more predominantly in the Western world and among the middle class. It is usually based on two generations where the group members are related by marriage. The term *family* refers to parents and children, and essentially, it dissolves with the death of a spouse. Societies based on nuclear families are places where employees are much more apt to pick up and move when a better career opportunity comes along. And the identity of individuals in these societies is more typically derived from one's immediate family and from one's vocation rather than from the heritage of one's extended family. Nuclear-family systems place a great deal of value on parent-child relationships, husband-wife relationships, and sibling relationships. Family systems play a profound role in the choices employees make and the things that motivate potential markets.

Understanding the colliding approaches to family life is becoming increasingly relevant to how we lead. Of all the cultural systems, the family system is widely regarded as the single most important system to understand, but this information often feels irrelevant to many organizational leaders.[8] Consider why some basic knowledge of these kinds of differences would help an American leader trying to negotiate a contract with a business owned by an ethnic Chinese family. Many of the most successful businesses in cities like Beijing, Jakarta, Kuala Lumpur, and Singapore are run by ethnic Chinese leaders who reflect a kinship approach to business. These companies are typically managed by the patriarch of the family who leads with unquestioned authority and is aided by a small group of family members and close subordinates. When the owner retires, the company is typically passed to the next generation. These businesses rarely relinquish control to outsiders and they usually put only family members on the board of directors.[9] Other multinational companies working in Middle Eastern contexts have learned the importance of hiring contractors connected to a local sheik's family in order to gain the sheik's cooperation and approval. These scenarios demonstrate the importance of understanding family systems for how we lead in varying contexts. The summary in Table 4-2 is something you can reference in the future to apply this understanding to your leadership.

Table 4-2.   Family Systems

Family Systems
The system a society develops for who can marry whom and the arrangements for how children and senior members are cared for.

Kinship:	Nuclear Family:
The family finds its identity in several generations of history and the household often includes three or more generations.	The family is based on two generations where the group members are related by marriage and consists primarily of parents and children.

Leadership Implications:
• Expect introductions in kinship societies to be embedded with references to siblings, uncles, parents, and grandparents. Learning about the career of an individual's parent may be very important. In contrast, introductions in nuclear-family societies are usually focused on one's vocational role and what one does for the organization. Conversations about family are considered "personal" and only appropriate after getting to know one another a bit better.
• When leaders from nuclear-family systems work with colleagues and employees from kinship-family systems, allowing room for family obligations will be important when recruiting and retaining talent from kinship societies.
• When leaders from kinship-family systems work with colleagues and employees from nuclear-family systems, beware that they may not see the importance of hearing or sharing about extended family relationships during an initial introduction.

Educational Systems: Formal vs. Informal

Societies also develop patterns for how their senior members transmit their values, beliefs, and behaviors to their offspring. These patterns are at the core of how societies develop systems for educating and socializing their young. Most of the world today is moving more toward formalized education where young people are socialized through schools, books, and professional teachers. But many cultures still place as much or more emphasis on the informal education of children from parents, older siblings, and extended family members. The use of rote teaching where students are expected to recite back information taught versus the development of analytical skills is an important point of difference among many educational approaches.

Leaders coming from Asia will often be frustrated with the perceived limitations among Westerners for memorizing and retaining information. They may see Westerners as struggling to synthesize individual parts into a whole. The same frustration occurs among Western leaders when their attempts at analysis are met with resistance from their cross-cultural counterparts. An understanding of the educational system in a particular culture can enhance the way you conduct meetings; develop partnerships; and market, train, and develop personnel. The summary in Table 4-3 is something you can reference in the future to apply this understanding to your leadership.

Legal and Political Systems: Formal Laws vs. Informal Governance

Most cultures develop systems for maintaining order to ensure citizens do not violate the rights of others in the society. This results in the legal system of a society, which is closely tied with the government of a particular place. In places like the United States, there's a formal legal system governed by a written constitution

Table 4-3.   Educational Systems

Educational Systems
The patterns for how the senior members of a culture transmit their values, beliefs, and behaviors to their offspring.

Formal:	Informal:
The use of schools, books, and professionally trained teachers to educate youth.	The emphasis on wisdom passed to youth from extended family members, parents, and siblings.

Leadership Implications:

- Develop and adapt training programs for employees with an understanding of the educational systems and preferences of people from various cultures. Some teaching methods may be very foreign or uncomfortable to individuals from certain cultures.
- Seek to understand the degree to which formal, academic research is valued as compared to conventional wisdom in the ways you motivate, negotiate, and market your work.
- When seeking to debunk a myth or advance a new idea, understand the primary source of socialization in a culture (e.g., sage wisdom versus academic research).

and through local, state, and federal laws. But while less formalized and complex, many smaller-scale, technologically simple societies also have effective ways of controlling behaviors.

Many businesses have become extremely frustrated in knowing how to maintain good working relationships among employees and with local officials because of ignorance about how the governing system works. One of the greatest mistakes made by leaders as they move in and out of various countries is assuming the government system works pretty much like it does at home. On the other hand, another typical response is assuming a legal system is corrupt or inferior because it's different. Understanding and respecting a society's legal system will significantly enhance the ability to effectively work in that culture.

It's also important to be aware that variations often occur even within a nation's given legal system. For example, the United States has some universal laws that govern the country, but there are numerous issues that get governed by individual states and cities. Many other countries have similar variations among different districts, provinces, and regions. In some contexts, laws apply differently to different ethnic groups within a society. For example, Malaysia, an Islamic state, has a different set of standards for its indigenous Malay citizens than it does for Chinese or Indian descent citizens. One U.S. company operating in Kuala Lumpur began offering yoga classes for employees during the lunch hour. The class was led by an American instructor as a way to offer employees holistic exercise. There was enthusiastic participation from several of the Indian and Chinese personnel; however, no Malays, the predominant population in the country and at this company, ever came to yoga. Eventually, the U.S. owners learned it's illegal for Malays to practice yoga because of the concern that elements of Hinduism in the ancient exercise could corrupt a Muslim's faith. Once again, a deep understanding of all the specific legal structures is not necessary for every leader, but an appreciation for the significance of how a legal system affects the way we work there is essential. Table 4-4 is something you can reference in the future to apply this understanding to your leadership.

Religious Systems: Rational vs. Mystical

Every culture develops a way of explaining what otherwise seems inexplicable. Why do bad things happen to good people? How come drunk drivers survive while innocent people get killed? Why do tsunamis kill some people while others escape? There are no uniform conventions for answering these questions, but all societies offer a variety of supernatural and religious beliefs for things

Table 4-4.   Legal Systems

Legal Systems
The systems developed by a society to protect citizens' rights.

Formal:	Informal:
A very formalized system, which is chronicled in things like a written constitution and laws.	Although less formalized, simple legal systems are still binding and are passed along through conventional wisdom. Citizens and visitors are presumed to understand and follow the rules.

Leadership Implications:
• Recruit local expertise to aid you in negotiating with legal and government officials.   • Take the time to learn which laws are relevant for your work in a respective place.   • Find out what unwritten practices should be used or avoided with legal officials. For example, giving a gift to a government official will be essential in some cultures but can get you arrested in another.

that go beyond human understanding. Admittedly, there are many differences within most cultures for how different individuals and their religions answer questions like these. One of the distinguishing differences between how many cultures organize their supernatural belief systems is rooted in the degree to which they take a rational, scientific approach to answering the inexplicable versus a more spiritual and mystical outlook on life. The rational approaches tend to place more emphasis on individual responsibility and work ethic while the more mystical views place a higher degree of confidence in supernatural powers, both good and evil.

Religious and supernatural beliefs can shape work-related attitudes in profound ways. Max Weber, often called the founder of sociology, analyzed the relationship between Protestantism and capitalism. Capitalism is driven in part by a Protestant work ethic, which is prevalent in Western societies and emphasizes hard work, diligence, and frugality with the aim of accumulating capital. It's assumed this approach will be the best for society. The guiding thought is: *A society won't survive without expecting people to work hard for it.*[10]

In contrast, Islam emphasizes charity to the poor and has rigorous measures to ensure profitable gains don't come at the expense of the poor. As a result, most Islamic banks prohibit charging interest on loans because gains from loans are seen as exploitive gains from the poor. Innovative businesses working in the Islamic context have factored in this reality by charging a fee up front rather than charging interest. Non-Islamic firms working in Islamic countries need to have a basic understanding of these Islamic practices.[11]

One U.S. business opened its Thailand office one flight above a Buddha statue. Only after several months of virtually no business did it learn that no one was coming to the office because the business violated a sacred rule: Never put yourself above Buddha, literally! After moving to a new location, business took off. Elsewhere, a Japanese multinational corporation was caught off guard by the degree to which religious beliefs affected its global expansion. The company decided to build a factory on a piece of land in rural Malaysia that was formerly a burial ground of the aboriginal people who had lived in the region. After building the factory, mass hysteria resulted among the factory workers of Malay origin. Many employees claimed they were inflicted with spirit possession. Putting the factory on former burial grounds was believed to have disturbed the earth and stirred the spirits, which then swarmed the factory premises.[12]

We can't underestimate the powerful role of religious beliefs and practices in how we work in different places. For Western leaders, who are often perceived to be Christian even if they aren't, a respectful conversation about some of the other great religions of the world will demonstrate significant respect when interacting with leaders from other parts of the world. You need not abandon your own religious convictions to convey honor and appreciation for the views and practices of others. This is a huge point to understand about cultural intelligence. We aren't interested in abandoning all our convictions, values, and assumptions. Instead, we're seeking to understand and respect the beliefs and priorities of others. The summary in Table 4-5 is something you can reference in the future to apply this understanding to your leadership.

Table 4-5.   Religious Systems

Religious Systems
The ways a culture explains the supernatural and what otherwise seems inexplicable.

Rational:	Mystical:
The emphasis is on finding reason-based scientific answers to the supernatural with a focus on individual responsibility and work ethic.	The emphasis is on supernatural powers, both good and evil, that control day-to-day events and life.

Leadership Implications:

- Be respectful about how you discuss your religious beliefs and learn what might be most likely to offend someone in light of the person's religious beliefs. Be alert to the most potentially offensive things that could be done in regard to a culture's religious beliefs and seek to avoid those practices.
- Become a student of how religious values and supernatural beliefs affect the financial, management, and marketing decisions made by an organization in a particular culture.
- Find out the key religious dates. Avoid opening a new business in China during the Festival of the Dead or on Diwali in India. Just as we wouldn't think of planning a key business meeting during Christmas in the Western world, learn what religious holidays to avoid in other locations.

Artistic Systems: Solid vs. Fluid

Finally, every society develops a system of aesthetic standards that get manifested in everything from decorative art, music, and dance to the architecture and planning of buildings and communities. There are many different ways we could examine artistic systems. One way of thinking about it is to observe the degree to which a society's aesthetics reflect clear lines and solid boundaries versus fluid ones. Many Western cultures favor clean, tight boundaries whereas many Eastern cultures prefer more fluid, indiscriminate lines.

In most Western homes, kitchen drawers are organized so that forks are with forks and knives are with knives. The walls of a room are usually uniform in color, and when a creative shift in color does occur, it usually happens at a corner or along a straight line midway down the wall. Pictures are framed with straight edges, molding covers up seams in the wall, and lawns are edged to form a clear line between the sidewalk and the lawn. Why? Because we view life in terms of classifications, categories, and taxonomies. And cleanliness itself is largely defined by the degree of order that exists. It has little to do with sanitation and far more to do with whether things appear to be in their proper place.

Maintaining boundaries is essential in the Western world; otherwise categories begin to disintegrate and chaos sets in.[13] Most Americans want dandelion-free lawns and roads with clear lanes prescribing where to drive and where not to drive. Men wear ties to cover the adjoining fabric on the shirts that they put on before going to the symphony, where they listen to classical music based on a scale with seven notes and five half steps. Each note has a fixed pitch, defined in terms of the lengths of the sound waves it produces.[14] A good performance occurs when the musicians hit the notes precisely.

In contrast, many Eastern cultures have little concern in everyday life for sharp boundaries and uniform categories. Different colors of paint may be used at various places on the same wall. And the paint may well "spill" over onto the window glass and ceiling. Meals are a fascinating array of ingredients where food is best enjoyed when mixed together on your plate. Roads and driving patterns are flexible. The lanes ebb and flow as needed depending on the volume of traffic. In a place like Cambodia or Nigeria, the road space is available for whichever direction a vehicle needs it most, whatever the time of day. And people often meander along the road in their vehicles the same way they walk along a path.

There are many other ways aesthetics between one place and another could be contrasted. But the important point is some basic understanding of how cultures differ within the realm of aesthetics. Soak in the local art of a place and chalk it up to informing your strategy for international business. The summary in Table 4-6 will help you apply aesthetic understanding to your leadership.

Table 4-6.   Artistic Systems

Artistic Systems	
A society's approach to aesthetics in everything from decorative art, music, and architecture to city planning.	
Clear:	Fluid:
A preference for clean, tight boundaries that emphasize precision and straight lines.	A preference for more fluid, indiscriminate lines with an emphasis on ebb and flow and flexibility.
Leadership Implications:	
• Determine whether you need to alter the color schemes, navigation logic, and representations on your website for various regions. What might seem like a clear navigation approach in your culture might be very confusing in another place. • Beware of assuming that symbols or logos can be universally applied in all cultural contexts. Do your homework to find out how symbols will be received in the places where you work. • Learn what cultural icons are revered. For example, inappropriate use of lions or the Great Wall when marketing to Chinese will erode credibility.	

Understanding these basic cultural systems and some overarching ways they function across various cultures is a key part of CQ knowledge. Though visible, it's easy to miss the importance and relevance of these systems if we don't take time to consider them. And as demonstrated with the iceberg diagram (see Figure 4-1), there will always be individuals within a culture who stray from the cultural norms for aesthetics or any of these cultural systems.

Conclusion

CQ knowledge begins with understanding culture's role on people's thoughts, attitudes, and behaviors. It's discerning what's universal to all humans, what's attributable to specific cultures, and what's idiosyncratic to individuals. Then we need to gain a basic grasp of the systems developed by cultures to deal with economics, family, education, legal issues, religion, and artistic expression. In Chapter 5, we'll look at two more ways to develop CQ knowledge: learning cultural values and language.

CHAPTER 5

DIG BENEATH THE TERRAIN: CQ KNOWLEDGE
(STEP 2B)

The journey toward enhanced cultural intelligence continues. CQ knowledge is the second step of the four-step cycle toward cultural intelligence. As described in Chapter 4, CQ knowledge refers to our level of understanding about culture and the ways cultures differ. Chapter 4 reviewed two ways to develop CQ knowledge—(1) see culture's role in yourself and others, and (2) review the basic cultural systems. This chapter explains two more ways to develop CQ knowledge—(3) learn the core cultural values, and (4) understand different languages.

Learn the Core Cultural Values

You'll undoubtedly see a connection between what a culture values and the cultural systems (e.g., economic, aesthetic, legal) reviewed in Chapter 4. Cultural values are what get emphasized most when teaching people about cross-cultural leadership. How do people in Mexico approach time or authority as compared with people in Germany? Although cultural values are just one factor in being an effective leader in our multicultural world, they are a significant part of building our CQ repertoire.

Given the abundance of books devoted to describing these values, we'll just briefly look at a few of the cultural values with the most relevance for leaders. Cultural values have the greatest relevance when juxtaposed against our personal orientation in these same values. We're going to look at five scales used to understand and measure cultural differences between one nation and another: time, context, individualism, power distance, and uncertainty avoidance. In my experience, these are the most helpful ones for developing CQ knowledge within the leadership context. These cultural values reflect national stereotypes of how many people from a respective country function. Stereotypes, while potentially dangerous, are a good starting point as long as they are descriptive and not judgmental. If we're open to expecting variability among different people from the same culture (e.g., some Mexicans are typically punctual and task oriented while most are more interested in relationships than in being on time), neutral stereotypes based on the cultural values that follow are worthwhile. This is one of the ways to address the challenge issued earlier—discerning between what's cultural and what's personal. A sampling of where several countries fall in these five values is provided in Table 5-1.

Table 5-1.   Cultural Values of Regions and Nations[1]

Country or Region	Time Orientation	High vs. Low Context	Individualism	Power Distance	Uncertainty Avoidance
Arab Countries	Event	High	38	80	68
Australia	Clock	Low	90	36	51
Brazil	Event	High	38	69	76
Canada	Clock	Low	80	39	48
China	Clock	High	20	78	37
East Africa Region	Event	High	27	64	52
France	Clock	Mid	72	68	86
Great Britain	Clock	Mid	89	35	35
Hong Kong	Clock	High	25	68	29
India	Event	High	48	77	40
Israel	Event	Low	54	13	81
Japan	Clock	High	46	54	92
Malaysia	Event	High	26	104	36
Mexico	Event	High	30	81	82
Russia	Clock	High	38	95	97
Singapore	Clock	High	20	74	NA
South Africa	Clock	High	65	49	49
Thailand	Clock	High	20	64	64
United States	Clock	Low	91	40	46

NOTE: Scores are on a scale of 1 to 120; 120 is the highest degree of the value listed (e.g., 120 in Individualism would be an extremely individualist culture and 1 an extremely collectivist culture).

Event Time vs. Clock Time

Some North Americans often say things like, "She's on *Latin* time!" And it's usually said with a pejorative tone. Change the word *Latin* for any number of other cultures that don't share the industrial world's obsession with punctuality and you can infer what that statement means. The Western world has a long history of defining success in light of how much gets produced and consumed. As a result, people in Western, industrialized cultures live by *clock time*. Punctuality and efficiency rule the day. The clock is what determines when things start and end. Respect, excellence, and conscientiousness are all communicated by punctuality.

In contrast, other cultures are far more interested in emphasizing the priority and obligation of social relationships. These cultures are often referred to as *event time* cultures. Events begin and end when all the participants feel the time is right rather than artificially imposing clock time. Spontaneity is a core value among individuals from these contexts.

We're all pretty familiar with these kinds of differences. The challenges that result from encountering someone with a different time orientation go far beyond punctuality, however. It comes right into how we collaborate and plan with other leaders cross-culturally. Marcelo is the leader of a large organization in Brazil. He and I had been working on developing a leadership-training program for several of his managers. We had a chance for a brief meal together while we were both attending a conference in Amsterdam. Marcelo is a large man with bulging brown eyes, thick dark hair, and a gregarious personality. We only had an hour to eat and talk before I needed to catch a train to the Schiphol Airport. After several minutes of hearing about his family, I attempted to transition toward some needed clarity about when we were going to launch the training program we had been working toward. Marcelo kept telling me about his daughter Renata, raving about the bread and cheese we were eating, and asking about my kids. I kept trying to gently circle back to nailing him down on a launch date, to which I only received vague, ambiguous responses.

It's not like I was totally unaware of what was going on, yet neither was I accomplishing what I felt we needed to clarify. But an understanding of the different ways we view time was a key point of understanding. I set myself up for an unrealistic expectation to try to get Marcelo to work on a scheduling issue when we just barely had enough time to catch up together socially.

The difference in time orientation is most evident across varying national cultures. But organizational cultures also have different ways they value time. Bearing in mind that various cultures are oriented differently toward time is another way to build our CQ knowledge. Note the summary in Table 5-2.

High Context vs. Low Context

After leaving my quick lunch with Marcelo, I was headed to the airport. Schiphol Airport is made for a traveler like me. Clear signage is everywhere, which reflects a value orientation called *low context.* A low-context culture is a place where little is left to assumption so things are spelled out explicitly. In contrast, *high-context* cultures are places where people have significant history together and so a great deal of understanding can be assumed. Things operate in high-context cultures as if everyone there is an insider and knows how to behave. Written instructions and explicit directions are minimal because most people know what to do and how to think.

Our families are probably the most tangible examples we have of high-context environments. After years of being together, we know what the unspoken rules are of what to eat, how to celebrate holidays, and how to communicate with each other. Many of our workplaces are the same. We know when to submit check requests, how to publicize an event, and how to dress on "casual" Fridays. New employees joining these kinds of organizations can really feel

Table 5-2.   Event vs. Clock Time

Value	Event Time Orientation	Clock Time Orientation
Description	Emphasizes social relationship Values spontaneity	Emphasizes punctuality, being industrious Values efficiency
Examples	Brazil India United Arab Emirates	Australia China United States

Leadership Implications:

- For those coming from clock time cultures, be willing to spend time building long-lasting relationships. Create margin and flexibility in your schedule for this pursuit.
- For those coming from event time cultures, be alert to the urgency felt by bringing closure and expediency. Find ways to communicate your need for more time while offering some concrete deadlines.
- Learn whether a culture with whom you're working is more focused on the past, present, or future.

lost without adequate orientation. And many religious services are also very high context. People routinely stand, bow, or recite creeds that appear very foreign and confusing to someone just joining a religious community for the first time. Discerning whether a culture provides direct and explicit communication versus one that assumes a high degree of shared understanding is a strategic point of knowledge. And leaders need to bear in mind the areas of their own organizational and national culture that are high context and how that affects outsiders when they enter.

In high-context places such as Latin America, Korea, and the Middle East, information is much more likely to be assumed and embedded within people rather than explicitly stated. There aren't a lot of signs or detailed information about how to act. High-context cultures are sometimes difficult places to visit as an outsider. This is one of the reasons why the socializing and sightseeing we discussed as part of developing CQ drive is so important. Learning how a culture tells its story and observing what it chooses to emphasize offers outsiders a glimpse into a place where a great deal is assumed.

Most national cultures across Europe and North America are categorized as low-context cultures. Many of our connections with particular people and places are of a shorter duration; therefore less is assumed. Instructions about where to park, how to flush the toilet, and where to order your food are often displayed. Low-context cultures can be easier to enter than high-context cultures, because even if you're an outsider, much of the information needed to participate is explicit. Extra attention is given to providing information about how to act. Note the summary in Table 5-3.

Individualism vs. Collectivism

Peter was one of six Australians being sent by a Sydney-based marketing firm to establish a branch office in Shanghai. The six Aussies had a variety of skill sets including Web design, graphic arts, and writing ability. Initially, Peter was appointed as the regional director for the Shanghai office. Even though the six marketing consultants were Aussies, Peter was committed to hiring local staff to fill some of the support roles. And given that his own vocational interests were more oriented toward the creative side of things, he wanted to find someone locally to become the office manager with the potential of moving that individual into the role of regional director.

Six months after Peter moved to China, I interviewed him. Peter has a larger-than-life personality that makes you feel like you're a long-lost mate as soon as you meet him. He began telling me about his commitment to hire local talent, but he felt like he was at a dead end. He had managed to hire a few support staff to help with clerical and administrative tasks but he couldn't find anyone to seriously

Table 5-3. Low vs. High Context

Value	Low Context	High Context
Description	Emphasizes explicit words Values direct communication	Emphasizes roles and implicit understanding Values indirect communication
Examples	United States Israel Australia	Brazil China United Arab Emirates

Leadership Implications:
- For individuals from low-context cultures, beware of ridiculing a place that just "doesn't bother" to label its roads or provide explicit instructions.
- For individuals from high-context cultures, be sensitive when hosting low-context individuals by providing more explicit instructions than what would ordinarily be needed with a colleague from your own culture.
- Find a way to get the understanding and communication needed. Develop a strategy for finding your way.

consider the office manager role. He knew he was offering a better salary and benefits package than what many other firms in Shanghai were paying. And he was explicit with job prospects about his interest in moving the person hired for this role into the regional director position. He had been given lots of good leads that led him to a number of people he would have gladly hired. Although each individual he contacted expressed appreciation for being considered, they all preferred to stay with their current employers.

The cultural value of individualism versus collectivism might explain what's going on here. Australia is one of the most individualistic cultures in the world. Employees in individualistic cultures like Australia, the United States, and the United Kingdom are expected to pursue every opportunity that comes along to get a better job with better pay. These cultures are largely governed by a commitment to do what's best for the individual as long as it doesn't infringe on the rights of other individuals. Peter was sure one of these interviewees would jump at this opportunity. In contrast to Australia, China is the most collectivist culture in the world. Collectivist cultures emphasize dedication and loyalty to the group, including the family "group," the religious "group," and the employment "group." The Chinese worker gives a high degree of loyalty to his or her employer and, in turn, expects support and loyalty back from the company, although the increasing talent crisis in China is beginning to challenge this value. Here again is a form of *guanxi*. The commitment is to what's best for the group. I've had Chinese friends tell me how their entire upbringing was filled with messages from their parents, who continually told them things like, "The one who stands out from the group is like a sore thumb sticking up and it will get chopped off! Blend in. Don't embarrass the family by sticking out!"

In addition, collectivist cultures are usually places where saving face is a high value. The fear of losing face or feeling shame is as innate to collectivist cultures as breathing is. It's a guiding force behind most interactions, or at the very least, it's the principle on which decisions are made as to what decisions are appropriate. Peter later contacted me and told me he found a creative way to approach his impasse in hiring support staff. He developed a partnership with a Shanghai-based company that offered the kind of services Peter and his colleagues needed. The Shanghai-based company agreed that at some point, Peter's firm may pursue hiring one of its employees and become that person's employer. He found an administrative whiz through this partnership who wasn't forced to become disloyal while talking with Peter about the potential of moving into the office manager role.

When McDonald's began opening restaurants in India, another

very collectivist culture, it soon learned it had to adapt its employee-of-the-month program. Being singled out with rewards for excellent work is a strong motivator for many in individualist cultures. But it's a demotivating factor in a place where you're socialized to blend in. McDonald's wisely adapted its motivational program toward being the team or restaurant of the month. Understanding the primary source of identity—the individual or the group—is an insight that will determine cross-cultural effectiveness.

The majority of the world is collectivist, but the majority of business and leadership literature is written by and for individualists. So it's easy to presume that individualist perspectives are more normative. But the reverse is true. Understanding the implications of this cultural value is essential for growing our CQ knowledge. Note the summary in Table 5-4.

Low vs. High Power Distance

Let me explain the next cultural value, *power distance*, by taking you with me to India for a minute. One morning when I was preparing to start a three-day training module in Delhi, I had an interesting interaction with my host, Sagar.

Dave: Are the training materials all printed and ready, Sagar?

Sagar: Oh, yes! They're at the print shop next door. They just need to be brought here.

Dave: Oh, great! I'll run next door and get them.

Sagar: No, no. I'll send someone to get them.

Dave: That's kind of you, Sagar. But I don't mind at all. I can use the exercise after the long flight. It's no problem. I'll just run next door and come right back.

Sagar: Please wait here a while. We will drink tea and I'll have someone bring them to us.

Table 5-4.   Individualism vs. Collectivism

Value	**Individualism**	**Collectivism**
Description	Emphasizes "I" and individual identity Prefers individual decisions and working alone	Emphasizes "we" and group identity (e.g., family, work, group, organization, tribe) Prefers group decisions and working with others
Examples	United States Australia United Kingdom	China Colombia United Arab Emirates

Leadership Implications:

* Learn how to motivate your employees. Those coming from an individualist culture are likely to be motivated through individual incentives whereas those from collectivist cultures will be more motivated by seeing their work team succeed.
* Those from individualist cultures need to understand the importance of long-term relationships and third-party connections when working with individuals from collectivist ones.
* Those from collectivist cultures need to understand that a partnership with an organization from an individualist culture may well be developed primarily through one or two individuals.

What's going on here? Is Sagar just trying to be a gracious host? Should I insist on getting the materials or am I being too task oriented and missing that Sagar just wants to have tea together? Or is he just trying to save face and keep me from knowing they haven't even been printed yet? It may have been any of the above. Interpreting the many possibilities of what this kind of exchange looks like is the kind of dilemma we'll explore further as we look at CQ strategy. But as I debriefed this encounter with a couple of

Indian friends afterward, combined with some reading I did elsewhere, I began to see this conflict over picking up a print order may have primarily related to the differing views Sagar and I have about power distance.

It seems I wasn't sufficiently status conscious to suit Sagar. A high-power-distance culture views it as the lot of some individuals in life to courier materials and carry books while others are given the role of doing things like teaching or being an executive. For me to have gone and gotten my own things would have been a slight on Sagar, demonstrating he doesn't know how to take care of a guest teacher. And it's possible it may have been a slur on the importance of education itself. By the way, the materials did show up right on time.[2]

Power distance refers to how "far apart" leaders and followers feel from each other. Countries scoring high in power distance—such as Mexico, India, and Ghana—offer a great deal of formal respect to leaders. Titles and status are revered, leaders and followers are unlikely to socialize together, and subordinates are not expected to question their superiors. Power distance is the extent to which differences in power and status are expected and accepted. It reveals where the power lies and how it's structured.

Again, this value varies not only in national cultures but also across other cultural contexts including generational subcultures, professional cultures, and organizational cultures. When visiting a new organization, notice how people address the people to whom they report, what kinds of titles are used, and how they're displayed. How are you introduced to the senior leader and what does the office setup suggest about power dynamics? Don't miss these important observations when you're in the interviewing process with a new organization or when you're courting a client in a new cultural context.

Individuals from high-power-distance cultures who come to work in the United States often demonstrate their discomfort with the different attitudes toward authority figures compared to what they see at home. An engineer from India said, "The first time my supervisor told me, 'I don't know,' I was shocked. I asked myself,

'Why is he in charge?' In my country, a superior would give a wrong answer rather than admit ignorance."

An international student from Indonesia, another culture scoring very high in power distance, made this comment about her experience coming to study at a U.S. university: "I was surprised and confused when on leaving Whittier Hall the provost held the door for me. . . . I was so confused that I could not find the words to express my gratefulness, and I almost fell on my knees as I would certainly do back home. A man who is by far my superior is holding the door for me, a mere student and a nobody."[3]

The United States is by no means the lowest on the scale of power distance. With 1 as the lowest level of power distance and 120 as the highest, the U.S. score is 40, and trailing behind are Canada, Germany, and Finland. The countries of Austria and Israel, with respective scores of 11 and 13, score lowest in power distance. In these low-power-distance contexts, followers feel at ease socializing with their leaders and addressing them as peers. Subordinates feel free to question their managers and they expect to have input in the decision-making process.

In Chapter 1, I suggested one of the primary reasons leaders need cultural intelligence is because we have to adapt our leadership style as we move across different cultures. My preference is to lead and be led with a participative style that reflects low power distance. I'm not a big fan of using formal titles, and for me, the flatter the organizational chart the better. But as I come to understand the way my culture's low power distance shapes my leadership preferences, it's also helping me see how high power distance shapes the preferred styles of leadership among others. Subordinates in high-power-distance cultures like India expect leaders to tell them exactly what to do. At the very least, if I insist on using a more empowering, participative style of leadership in India, I have to creatively figure out how to make that work and I need to accept that multiple leadership styles can be effective.

Considering the relationship between so-called high-status

people and low-status people, and between leaders and followers, is an important area we need to understand. Leaders who engage in cultural intelligence will avoid writing off a leadership style they observe cross-culturally, but instead will seek to understand it. This understanding will prepare us for some of the ways we'll adjust our behavior when we get to the fourth step of CQ action. Note the summary in Table 5-5.

Low vs. High Uncertainty Avoidance

The last cultural value for our discussion is *uncertainty avoidance.* This is the extent to which most people in a culture are at ease with the unknown. Cultures scoring high on uncertainty avoidance are places where people are uncomfortable with ambiguity and risk. They have little tolerance for the unknown. People living in these kinds of cultures focus on ways to reduce uncertainty and ambiguity, and they create structures to help ensure some measure of predictability. For example, someone leading staff primarily from the dominant cultures in Greece, Japan, or France would be wise to give very clear instructions and timetables for when and how they want a work assignment completed. Simply telling an employee to write a plan in order to competently address the problem would create all kinds of dissonance for a team member oriented toward high uncertainty avoidance.

On the other hand, cultures scoring lower in uncertainty avoidance, such as Britain, Jamaica, and Sweden, are not as threatened by unknown situations and what lies ahead. Open-ended instructions, varying ways of doing things, and loose deadlines are more typical in these kinds of cultures. These are places where ambiguity and unpredictability are welcomed. Strict laws and rules are resisted and people are more accepting of opinions different from theirs.

Uncertainty avoidance is also a way to understand the differences that exist between two cultures that might otherwise seem to be much the same. For example, Germany and Great Britain have

Table 5-5.   Low vs. High Power Distance

Value	Low Power Distance	High Power Distance
Description	Expects that all should have equal rights Is willing to question and challenge the views of superiors	Expects power holders to be entitled to privileges Is willing to support and accept the views of superiors
Examples	Israel Austria United Kingdom [United States is almost in the middle between low and high power distance]	China United Arab Emirates France

Leadership Implications:

- Learn how to motivate your employees. Those coming from an individualist culture are likely to be motivated through individual incentives whereas those from collectivist cultures will be more motivated by seeing their work team succeed.
- Those from individualist cultures need to understand the importance of long-term relationships and third-party connections when working with individuals from collectivist ones.
- Those from collectivist cultures need to understand that a partnership with an organization from an individualist culture may well be developed primarily through one or two individuals.

a great deal in common. Both are in Western Europe, both speak a Germanic language, both had relatively similar populations before the German reunification, and the British royal family is of German descent. Yet, the person who understands the uncertainty-avoidance dimension will quickly notice considerable differences between life in Frankfurt and life in London. Punctuality, structure, and order are modus operandi in German culture, whereas Brits are much more easygoing regarding time and deadlines and they tend to be less concerned about precision than Germans. This can be explained in part by the different views the cultures have toward the unknown. Beware. As continually noted, we can't make blanket assumptions about how all Brits or Germans view uncertainty and risk. These cultural values are just one aspect of applying cultural intelligence. But they're a helpful place to begin anticipating how our leadership might unfold when encountering differing degrees of tolerance for ambiguity and the unknown.

I've taught in Singapore more than I've taught almost anywhere in the world. Some studies have erroneously labeled Singapore as low in uncertainty avoidance. That would mean Singaporeans, like the British, enjoy ambiguity and open-ended conclusions. Although Singapore is cosmopolitan and allows for many value orientations, on the whole, the dominant culture in Singapore has a low-risk orientation that gets measured as having high uncertainty avoidance.[4] It's not uncommon for me to be asked twelve to fifteen times in advance of teaching a group of Singaporeans to provide another level of clarity about what I'll be covering in an upcoming seminar. Even after I provide as explicit an explanation as I know how, I'm often asked for more clarification. Similarly, when living there, my wife and I were often cautioned by Singaporean parents against allowing our kids to freely climb up and down the playground equipment in the park. It seemed the cultural aversion to risk caused them to be extremely cautious with the ways they would allow their children to play. Whether it is investing, exploring different faith traditions, or teaching methodologies, the traditional orientation of the Singaporean culture is much more comfortable with boundaries and predictable certainty. A highly involved government with lots of laws is often viewed by Singaporeans as a small price to pay for safety and certainty. Note the summary in Table 5-6.

Leaders with assumptions like Jeff's, the American business guy

Table 5-6.   Low vs. High Uncertainty Avoidance

Value	Low Uncertainty Avoidance	High Uncertainty Avoidance
Description	Prefers few rules, little structure, and few guidelines Tolerates unstructured and unpredictable situations	Prefers written rules, structure, and guidelines Is uncomfortable with unstructured or unpredictable situations
Examples	Jamaica Sweden Malaysia [China and the United States are near the middle on this value]	Greece United Arab Emirates Japan

Leadership Implications:
- When working with individuals with low uncertainty avoidance, work to minimize ambiguity and related anxiety about the future. Be explicit regarding objectives and deadlines. Make modest proposals for change with a well-communicated strategy.
- When working with individuals with high uncertainty avoidance, avoid dogmatic statements and being highly rigid. Invite them into the adventure and in exploring the unknown.

who was convinced "people are people and business is business," are unable to effectively sustain collaborative work that involves people from diverse cultures. In many cases, the failure of a leader to understand the profound differences between things like an individualist approach to life and work and a collectivist one results in a career that plateaus or moves backward. In contrast, leaders who grow in CQ knowledge are able to understand how cultural values shape performance outcomes.

By referring back to Table 5-1, you can see an overview of how several cultures vary across the five cultural values we just examined. Undoubtedly you're seeing your own tendency in each of these values, too. These cultural values can help us answer the questions we should ask when moving through the second step of the CQ cycle. There's one more way to develop CQ knowledge: *language.*

Understand Different Languages

A few years ago, the Dairy Association led a wildly successful marketing campaign throughout the United States built on the slogan "Got Milk?" Unfortunately, when the campaign was exported to Mexico, the translation read, "Are you lactating?"[5] There are countless other examples like this one. A U.S. software company suffered from having the name of its industry translated as an "underwear" company when launching internationally. A European company couldn't succeed at selling its chocolate and fruit dessert called "Zit" in the United States nor could the Finns who attempted to sell "Super Piss," a Finnish product for unfreezing car door locks. These examples are humorous but the challenge of language goes beyond funny translations. Microsoft experienced a great deal of resistance from many regions around the world in response to its icon "My Computer." The assumed implication of private ownership, which is uncommon in cultures without private property and ownership protection, caused a great deal of angst for affiliates and consumers in places that are more collectivist in nature.[6] This is an example of how a cultural value like individualism versus collectivism shapes language and has an impact on real practice.

Read almost any book on effective leadership, and you'll see a recurring theme in regard to the essential role of consistent, clear communication. Communication—whether creating a marketing campaign, drafting a memo, or casting a vision—is ubiquitously tied to culture. Some say language and culture are one and the same, pointing to the reality that Eskimos have lots of different words for snow and very few to describe tropical fruits. The reverse is true in some tropical contexts. Language and culture evolve together as people live in relationship to their surroundings. As we grow in CQ knowledge, we need to understand some basic things about communication and language and their relationship to culture.

Some U.S.-based organizations flippantly quip, "English is becoming the lingua franca of international business." But in actuality, English is just one of the major languages of world trade and the mother tongue of only 5 percent of the world's population.[7] Leaders who speak more than one language have an advantage over those who don't because when you're fluent in a language, speaking and *thinking* in that language becomes an automatic, subconscious action. Not only can we more easily communicate with others who speak that language, we also gain a heightened way of seeing how they label the world. It provides a way to understand what's going on that is much harder to grasp when done through translation. Jaguar, the British automobile maker, discovered the importance of language when it began in-house German language studies to help increase the company's competition in Germany against local competitors, Mercedes and BMW. A year after doing so, its sales in Germany jumped 60 percent.[8]

If you speak only one language, consider signing up for an introductory foreign language course or hiring a tutor. Chances are, you won't have to look far to find someone who can teach you the basics. While becoming fluent is a great ideal, just the process of learning another language significantly contributes to growth in CQ knowledge. You might find yourself innovating and leading in new ways simply as a result of learning a new language.

Language understanding can be an issue even when working within another English-speaking context. Different expressions and terms are frequent points of confusion among Americans, Brits, Indians, and Aussies, just to name a few.

And similar kinds of communication challenges exist when

moving from one organization or profession to the next. An academic talking with a group of business executives needs to translate academic language into terms that communicate effectively in that corporate context. I often encounter people who work in professional cultures that are unfamiliar to me, like medical professionals, biochemists, or automotive manufacturers. I immediately observe the difference between the cultural intelligence of those individuals who can talk to me about their work using language I can understand versus others who use all kinds of trade lingo that means nothing to me. Doctors and nurses with CQ knowledge have to adjust their verbal and nonverbal language when talking about a diagnosis with family members versus doing so with medical peers. With CQ knowledge, we understand that our words stem from a variety of the cultural contexts that shape who we are. With that comes a great deal of assumed meaning. As we'll see further in step three of the Cultural Intelligence Cycle—CQ strategy—enhanced understanding about culture helps us monitor whether others can make sense of what we're saying based on the words we're using to express it.

I was recently involved with a ten-year-old nonprofit organization. It had enjoyed a high level of success in reaching its performance goals for the first seven years of its existence. But the organization's activity and bottom line had been in steady decline for the last two years. One of the things observed in talking with several of the staff and constituents was an unusual aversion toward anything that sounded "corporate" or institutional. In fact, one business leader who observed the organization described it as having antibodies in its system to anything that sounded remotely corporate. The board of directors for this organization was in the midst of seeking a new CEO. Part of applying cultural intelligence to the culture of this nonprofit organization was to change the title of the primary leader being sought from CEO to team leader. Of course, if the only change made was in the title on the job description, the aversion toward corporate culture would be addressed only for a moment. But this shift in language was the first step toward developing a leadership plan that uniquely suited the ethos of this organization, expressed in a language that resonated with who they were.

Communication, both formal and informal, is the most important leadership practice. Many of the problems that occur in an organization are the direct result of people failing to communicate in ways that truly enhance understanding. Learning appropriate language for a cultural context provides the understanding necessary for flexing our communication, something we'll revisit in the fourth step of CQ action.

Conclusion

Notice the reflections written by this North American traveling in Peru, South America:

> We flew into Iquitos from Lima last night. The challenges began as soon as we landed. . . . The airport looked like a dilapidated barn. But they sure took baggage security seriously. They wouldn't let us have our bags until they checked the tags. *I guess they have to do that here; otherwise people would steal them.*
>
> We're supposed to meet the Peruvian hosts at 9. But *people aren't very punctual here.* Maybe they need a good time management seminar.
>
> *What I wouldn't give to have something normal tonight!* A good burger, an ice-cold drink, and a salad would taste so great. Instead I expect another round of beans and rice. . . .

Whether the pleas for "normal food" come from my daughter or from a colleague with whom I'm traveling, I'm not fazed anymore by these kinds of ethnocentric statements. They get said continually. But reading this journal threw me because the traveler who wrote these statements was me! I recently found this journal

I wrote as an eighteen-year-old. It was my first sojourn abroad. My daughter Emily got a good laugh when I told her I was saying things at eighteen that she stopped saying before she was eight.

Cultural ignorance need not be a permanent condition. That's the really encouraging thing. We can all grow in the degree to which we understand culture. The starting point for CQ knowledge is understanding how culture shapes thinking and behavior. It's understanding what's universal, what's cultural, and what's personal. And we develop CQ knowledge by understanding cultural systems, values, and language.

BEST PRACTICES FOR CQ KNOWLEDGE

1. *Study a foreign language.* You probably won't need to look far to find a teacher. Native speakers are usually the best teachers. Even learning a few phrases goes a long way when we travel abroad.

2. *Read international novels and memoirs.* Books like this one provide a conceptual framework for thinking about culture, but there's something far more visceral about reading a novel like *The Kite Runner* or watching a movie like *Crash* to build CQ knowledge. Enter another world through novels, memoirs, and movies set in another place. Visit www. davidlivermore.com for suggestions.

3. *Be globally informed.* Tap into various news sources to get beyond the latest gossip about Hollywood celebrities. BBC World News is one of the finest sources along with www. worldpress.org. And try visiting Al Jazeera's website to see how the same events are described in very different ways. When traveling, pick up something other than *USA Today* to get a local perspective.

4. *Gain some basic insights about where you're going.* Although expertise about cultural specifics is not the primary thrust of CQ knowledge, visiting sites like http://news.bbc. co.uk/2/hi/country_profiles/default.stm can be helpful. The goal is to get a basic overview of a country, its history, and the key issues facing its people so that at least there's a place to begin conversations while there.

5. *Go to the grocery store.* Looking at the products and layout of a grocery store in ethnically different communities can be a fascinating way to observe some cultural differences. Beware of making assumptions based on what you see, but do observe what is the same and what is different from where you shop.

CHAPTER 6

TURN OFF THE CRUISE CONTROL: CQ STRATEGY

(STEP 3)

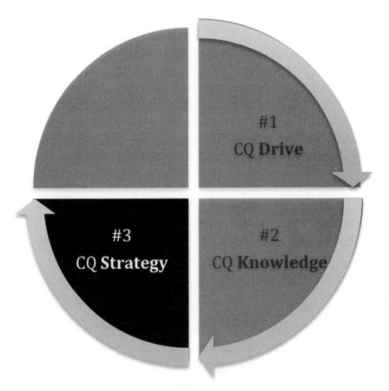

STEP 3: CQ STRATEGY: How should I plan?	
Strategizing and making sense of culturally diverse experiences	
Profile of a leader with high CQ strategy:	Leaders with high CQ strategy develop ways to use cultural understanding to develop a plan for new cross-cultural situations. These leaders are better able to monitor, analyze, and adjust their behaviors in different cultural settings. They are conscious of what they need to know about an unfamiliar culture.

I'm not interested in simply researching and writing about cultural intelligence. I want to apply it to my own leadership practice. But there are many times when I still appear culturally ignorant. For example, my attempt to find out whether Dr. Jones was a crook (see Chapter 1) was rooted in my North American orientation toward direct and explicit communication. I have little tolerance for dodging the elephant in the room and while I surely value diplomacy, at the end of the day, my modus operandi is to address conflict directly. When I arrived at the Monrovia airport, I was able to step back and see that Tim, the Liberian American visiting for two weeks, and his porter were missing each other. I could listen to the stories of my breakfast companions' mishaps with baby food and medical shipments. But I failed to take the time to think about how my direct name-the-elephant-in-the-room approach would work in Liberia.

If you had asked me about some of the values found in Liberian culture, I could have quickly talked to you about the high level of loyalty and commitment given to relationships. I think I could have even described the value of saving face for a friend and colleague above the value of providing accurate information to a stranger from another country. But I failed to make use of my knowledge to effectively accomplish what I needed—a clearer understanding of whether we should partner with Dr. Jones and Madison College. Only as I stepped back and reflected on what happened, combined with Moses's commentary, did I begin to better understand that I was putting Dr. Harris in an impossible situation. The ability to connect our cultural understanding with how we actually lead is what we're getting at with CQ strategy. This conversation could have been more helpful if I had spent more time planning how to approach Dr. Harris with a contentious issue.

The next day, Moses and I were with another Liberian who used to teach at Madison College and consequently knew Dr. Jones, the alleged embezzler. Having spent some time thinking through the previous day's interaction with Dr. Harris, I used a very different approach. As compared with my direct, bottom-line approach that is more typical for me, this time I asked for many of the strengths about Dr. Jones and his school. At one point, Moses excused himself to take a phone call, so I asked the leader with whom we were meeting, "What might a school like ours find challenging in partnering with Dr. Jones's school?" I couched the question so he could offer feedback that wouldn't have to be considered a negative assessment of Dr. Jones and his school. The leader offered several points of caution, many of which closely aligned with the kinds of critiques Moses had been offering. His critique was still indirect but evident.

CQ strategy is what we do with the understanding we gain from CQ knowledge. It helps us go beyond the surface and dive into the subtle but powerful issues that often make or break our leadership. As a result, CQ strategy is the key link between our cultural understanding and behaving in ways that result in effective leadership.

Driving is frequently used as a metaphor to explain CQ strategy. When I drive in cities and places familiar to me, I'm prone to multitasking. I might have the cruise control on and the radio playing while also carrying on a lively conversation with my travel companions or on my cell phone. But when I drive into a new city and need to find a destination, I slow down, turn off the radio, and minimize my conversation. Driving in a new place requires much more attentiveness. This is especially true if I'm in a place where they drive on the other side of the road. I feel more confident driving in new places if I've planned ahead to print off directions. Sometimes the computerized directions don't account for unexpected construction. So even when I plan ahead, I have to remain alert to see whether I'm moving toward my destination. You get the idea. This is what CQ strategy does for our leadership cross-culturally. It requires that we turn off the cruise control and become more conscious and alert about our surroundings in order to develop an appropriate strategy for a new cultural situation. Similar to what happens when we drive around an unfamiliar place, there are a variety of processes involved with CQ strategy. There are three important subdimensions to CQ strategy: *awareness, planning,* and *checking.*[1] These offer three important ways for growing our CQ strategy.

HOW TO DEVELOP CQ STRATEGY

Become more aware.

Plan your cross-cultural interactions.

Check to see if your assumptions and plans were appropriate.

Key question: What do I need to plan in order to do this cross-cultural assignment successfully?

Become More Aware

CQ strategy begins by simply slowing down the RPMs long enough to become consciously aware of what's going on internally and externally as we lead in a multicultural world. Awareness is stepping back from what we're doing and reflecting on it. It's disciplining ourselves to see what we otherwise miss. Awareness is one of the primary tools that enables us to discern between the three levels of the iceberg—what's universal, cultural, and personal? Awareness results in better decision making and overall performance.

Many religious traditions have a great deal to offer our understanding of awareness. For example, Buddhist scriptures urge followers to deliberately be still in order to become completely aware of what's occurring in body, mind, and consciousness. Buddhists are encouraged to apply this same kind of awareness to their surrounding environment in order to be fully "present."[2] Likewise, many Christian writers exhort believers to utilize contemplation as a way of tuning into themselves, others, and God. Christians use awareness to help subdue their vices and to live more virtuously.

In the cross-cultural context, awareness means moving out of some of the automated ways we do things in more familiar environments. Many of our day-to-day actions and leadership are things we do without even thinking about it. We develop semiautomatic habits and patterns of behaving as a way to simplify our lives. Most of us brush our teeth the same way every day. Even people who aren't multitaskers can easily watch the news or listen to a conversation while brushing their teeth. This same kind of semiautomatic behavior is at work on January 1 when we automatically write last year's date or when we flip on the turn signal in the car when approaching an intersection. Putting together an agenda for a staff meeting or writing a memo to all staff might not be quite as semiautomatic as these other examples, but after doing it several times, we all do leadership tasks like these without much conscious effort and thought.

However, as we become more self-aware, we learn the importance of shutting down some of our semiautomatic behavior when we're in a new context. I brush my teeth differently when I visit many parts of the developing world because my immune system isn't accustomed to the tap water there. We should also consider whether to alter some of our semiautomatic leadership tasks. Communicating something through a memo might work fine in the office at home but will it be the best way to communicate to personnel overseas? Or take the example of preparing a public presentation, something leaders often do. I'm not sure any of us would want to speak publicly without some awareness of what we're doing. But for those who speak regularly, we semiautomatically assess how our presentations are being received. We intuitively assess whether the audience is engaged and listening.

One study I conducted examined what happened when North American leaders traveled overseas to teach one-week workshops to local leaders in places throughout Africa and South America. Every one of the North American teachers described the eagerness of the local leaders for the training. The North American leaders were struck by how hungry the locals were for the material taught. Notice the contrast between what one North American trainer said compared with what one of the South Africans who sat through his training said:

North American trainer describing his teaching in South Africa:	*South African leader who sat in during the teaching:*
"They were so engaged. They sat and listened and they didn't get up and go to the bathroom every five minutes or constantly ask for breaks. The room was really hot and humid but that didn't seem to faze them. They were so respectful."	"I'm glad he felt respected. But he needs to realize we would never think about talking or getting up to leave in the middle of a lecturer's presentation. It would be unheard of for us to do that to a teacher, much less a foreign guest. It doesn't necessarily mean the content was engaging."

This trainer's assessment may have been accurate in a North American context but on the whole, the South African leaders who participated in the training gave very low marks to the relevance and value of the training they received from the North American leaders. With a heightened degree of awareness, these leaders could have paused to think about how to get accurate feedback.

Becoming aware is an active process of drawing on the cultural understanding derived from CQ knowledge to see culture's role in shaping a situation. It's shutting down our semiautomatic impulses, suspending our assumptions for a period of time, and remaining aware throughout our cross-cultural experiences.

Let's take a minute to do a two-part exercise to enhance our awareness. Grab a sheet of paper and create two columns, one labeled "Observations" and the other labeled "Interpretations." Look at the picture in Figure 6-1. Then, follow the directions in the table below it. In the left column, record your observations and in the right column, suggest interpretations for what you observe.

Figure 6-1.   Awareness of Observations vs. Interpretations

Awareness Exercise Part 1: *Observe*	*Awareness Exercise Part 2:* *Interpret*
In the left column, record only what you can actually see in the picture. Don't suggest what it means; just write down objective observations. How many people are in the picture? How are they dressed? What objects do you see? What décor is evident? What kind of expressions are on their faces? Resist explaining what you think they're doing and why. Only write down what anyone could see by looking at this picture. Don't rush through this part of the exercise. Part of moving toward CQ strategy requires that we slow down long enough to accurately observe what we see. Write down what you observe.	Now begin to think about the "why" questions that accompany *what* you observed. Where do you think these people are? What do you think they're doing? Are you sure? How do you think these individuals are connected to each other? What kind of mood do you think exists? Why is there one mug on the table? Why is the room decorated like this? You'll probably feel like you're guessing at some of this. You are. Write down your best guesses and interpretations as to why you think you observe what you do. If you were in this room, which individuals would you be naturally drawn to? Write down your interpretations.

To what degree are you confident about what you wrote in Part 1 compared to Part 2? You should be less certain about your answers to Part 2. Even the observations we make are profoundly shaped by our cultural background. The things we notice and how we identify them stem from our cultural orientation. But the interpretations behind those observations are especially influenced by our culture and personality. Appropriate observations may have included things like seeing two women, two men, three Caucasians, one Asian, one computer, one mug, three individuals seated and one standing, and everyone looking at the computer, and so forth. These are all observations we can agree on in light of what is in the picture. Interpretations can be all across the board but might include explanations for the kind of clothes being worn, the expressions on their faces, the decorations in the room, and the perceived relationships.

Interpreting events and behavior is hard enough in a familiar cultural context. But it's extremely difficult when we enter an unfamiliar environment. Awareness prepares us for the kinds of adaptations needed in most cross-cultural settings. I often run through this exercise in my head when I walk into a company's office for the first time to discuss a business proposal. I observe what's on the wall, the office setup, the way employees are dressed, and the titles used for various positions. Who gets invited to the meeting to discuss our proposal? These are all the Part 1 observations. Almost simultaneously while making those observations, I'm making Part 2 judgments and interpretations. Who holds the power? Who are the ultimate decision makers for this project? What are the vested interests behind the parties sitting at the table?

CQ strategy, the third step in the CQ cycle, is the way we answer the *why* questions behind what we experience and observe. *Why* does negotiation seem to consistently involve these dynamics here? *Why* is the leadership of this organization structured this way? *Why* is the office decorated like this? The first way to answer these why questions is by becoming more aware. Based on our understanding of people and culture, we interpret what's going on in a particular place. When we're in a familiar environment, this process occurs with little effort. We know how to greet a business colleague as compared to a close friend. We can sell something on the fly or express empathy to a subordinate without much conscious effort. If we have some level of emotional intelligence, we know how to approach conflict and how to communicate in a familiar context. But with heightened awareness, we realize all those things might need to be done differently in a new cultural context. The sarcastic humor that seems to enhance informality and collegiality in one organizational culture might erode trust in another. Turning down a dinner invitation could be a deal breaker in one cultural context and inconsequential in another.

Awareness is part of the overall CQ repertoire. It isn't a skill that only helps you in one place or situation; it can be applied in any cultural context. As we become more adept at awareness, we can take this skill further by intentionally being aware of ourselves and aware of others.

Self-Awareness

The first way we talked about enhancing CQ drive in Chapter 3 was by being honest with ourselves about our level of interest in a cross-cultural assignment. A similar kind of honest introspection is equally important to CQ strategy. If in Step 3 we continue the honest assessment started in Step 1, it will help us to develop appropriate plans for a cross-cultural task. Self-awareness isn't foreign territory for most leaders. In recent years, there's been a surge of leadership materials devoted to helping leaders become self-aware through tools like personality profiles and strength assessments. The discoveries we make through resources like these can help us grow in CQ strategy. For example, my top strength on Clifton's StrengthsFinder is "achiever," a characteristic of one who finds great satisfaction in hard work and productivity.[3] It's helpful for me to bear this in mind when I'm working in more laid-back cultures where relationships take priority over tasks. Through awareness, I have a better understanding of the personal frustration that often ensues when it feels like I haven't had a very productive day. I can also temper some of my frustration by redefining *productivity* in relational terms when working in more relationally driven cultures. With a heightened sense of awareness, we transcend merely being defined by our irritation or frustration and seek to understand what's behind it.

The degree to which we're self-aware as we lead and relate cross-culturally stems from our level of CQ knowledge about our own cultural contexts. And as we become aware of how our own behavior is shaped by culture, and of how others are likely to perceive us given our cultural background, we can begin to consciously accommodate for those perceptions. For example, it's one thing to understand that war and *Baywatch* are two predominant images many people around the world associate with Americans. But with awareness, American leaders can look for cues as to whether the non-American with whom they're interacting has that perception.

Self-awareness is more than just introspective naval gazing. It offers us greater control over the many hours and dollars we invest in working with affiliates around the world. Burnout and fatigue are among the top negative consequences leaders associate with the growing demand to work across a myriad of cultures and time zones. Self-awareness is a key strategy for fending off a great deal of the frustration, burnout, and fatigue that occur in cross-cultural work.

Other Awareness

As we gain an understanding of what's going on internally, we need to apply that same kind of awareness and understanding to others and to the environment around us. I've done ongoing research on the experiences of North Americans who volunteer overseas for one or two weeks. Most of these volunteers travel to developing countries where they help with disaster relief, build medical clinics, teach English, or engage in religious mission work. Of all the comments made by these North American travelers, the most common statement made upon their return is something like, "Even though those people have so little, *they're so happy!*" There's something endearing about hearing a group of relatively wealthy North Americans talk about their amazement that people with so little could be so happy. My question is, are the people they observed really happy? I've asked several hundred of these volunteers, "What makes you think they're happy?" They most often respond, "Because they were always smiling and laughing. And they were so generous to us. They fed us better than they eat themselves."

Part of becoming more aware of others requires we slow down to ask what familiar behaviors might mean in a different culture. The *observation* made by these American travelers is usually accurate—the locals they're meeting are in fact smiling and generous. But the question is whether the North Americans are accurately *interpreting* what those behaviors mean.

First, if you don't speak the language and you're just meeting someone for the first time, what do you do? After some feeble attempts at saying things like "Hola!" "Gross Got!" or "Nee how!" there's often some nervous laughter that ensues. It's really awkward. So the locals might be expressing happiness or their smiles might just be a nervous response.

Then add that in places like Thailand, where there are twenty-three different smiles, each smile communicates something different. And in one small, extremely polite community in New Zealand, smiling reactions are a way of expressing that they feel deeply offended.[4] As I've consistently said, the point isn't to learn every nuanced meaning. But with heightened awareness of others, an individual will realize that while smiles might reflect genuine happiness, they just as well might be a nervous cross-cultural response that indicates little about one's level of contentment. Awareness informed by CQ knowledge will help us make more accurate interpretations.

Here are some other ways to become more aware of a diverse workforce and customer base:

- Spend at least 50 percent of the time you have with your direct reports *listening*.
- Make regular appointments with your global partners "just" to hear their insights.
- Ask store employees in various places what's selling. Don't miss out on their frontline observations.
- Seek varied sources of input. Check out YouTube and see what people are watching from various parts of the world.
- Check out a variety of newspapers. What are the best-selling books and movies in London? In Dubai? In Moscow?
- Keep your eyes peeled for new trends in art, film, and theatre.

These practices can serve us well in our own environment too, but they're particularly valuable for becoming more aware in different contexts. Awareness isn't something that needs to take a great deal of time. It's a strategy we can use on the fly as we move in and out of various meetings, trips, and conversations. The simple discipline of seeing what we might otherwise miss is one of the best ways to develop CQ strategy.

Plan Your Cross-Cultural Interactions

Another way to grow our CQ strategy is to use the insights gained from our awareness to create new plans and strategies for how to do the same work in a different context. When I have to drive on the left side of the road rather than what I'm used to on the right, I have to remain very alert. But having done it several times, even if I'm driving in a brand-new place, it's easier than the first few times I did it. I've developed a few basic strategies for keeping track of what side I'm supposed to be on. Each new place brings with it some new rules and challenges to my driving, but the more I drive in different places, the more adept I become at using heightened awareness to get to my destination. Ironically, it sometimes begins to change the ways I go about driving back home, too. I find the same thing in my leadership strategies. Yet, it's surprising how often we'll spend thousands of dollars to travel twenty-four hours to the other side of the world without having spent any time planning how to make the most of our time there.

The real goal of CQ strategy is to take the things learned from tuning into the cultural understandings from one situation and to accurately apply them to other situations. I never seem to stop having disorienting and confusing encounters like the one I had in Liberia with Dr. Harris and Moses. But CQ strategy and planning helps me build on growing numbers of these situations and I learn how to better negotiate and lead in similar encounters.

Planning means anticipating how a task you do naturally at home might need to be altered when done with someone from a different cultural background. This can be as simple as mapping out a one-on-one meeting you have scheduled. Unless it's conflict laden, I don't usually spend a great deal of time planning out a one-on-one meeting with a colleague or subordinate in my home office. I might keep a running list of things to discuss but when we get together, we just move through them naturally. But we often need to spend additional time preparing for these same kinds of meetings when they involve individuals from a different cultural background. This doesn't have to take an inordinate amount of time and it shouldn't feel like it's manipulative. It's simply factoring in the time to anticipate how to most respectfully and effectively discuss the issues at hand. The planning for these kinds of encounters can be as easy as spending a few minutes en route to the meeting anticipating how to best address the issues you need to discuss. Ask yourself:

- What kind of small talk is appropriate for a person from this culture and for this individual?
- Who should initiate the transition from small talk into business?
- How will you get to action steps in this meeting?
- How much direction should you provide?

It's difficult to answer these questions without a growing measure of cultural understanding. Good CQ strategy requires good CQ knowledge.

A leader having high CQ strategy will actively create new strategies or adapt existing ones to deal with the new and unique aspects of an environment. This kind of leader is able to incorporate various observations and interpretations to create new strategies for new situations.[5] Most contexts provide ambiguous, at best, and often misleading cues about what is happening in an unfamiliar environment. That should be evident from the observation/interpretation awareness exercise we did earlier. As we become more aware, we can cautiously transfer our interpretations from one situation to another. We can't be too quick to assume similar situations are analogous but good planning will allow us to become more in tune with emerging patterns across diverse situations and contexts.

Check to See If Your Assumptions and Plans Were Appropriate

One more important way to develop CQ strategy is to seek out information to confirm or disconfirm whether our enhanced awareness and subsequent plans are appropriate. Western business executives need to be aware of when and how to speak up during meetings with Asians. Those with high CQ strategy will observe the interactions and communication style of their Asian counterparts, such as turn taking, and they will plan how and what to say before speaking up. Once they do so, they will work hard to monitor how their input is being received.[6] When you gain the ability and confidence to function at this high level of cognitive processing, it's highly rewarding and results in some of the best international practice. This comes easier to those who are adept at multitasking. The three-step process of awareness, planning, and checking usually happens simultaneously. The goal is to get more and more adept at remaining seamlessly aware of what's going on in yourself and others, to use that awareness to plan where to head next in the interaction, and to monitor whether your strategy is working.

In this process, it's really important for us to expect we'll misunderstand some things that happen as well as remain confused about others. At the very least, even a leader with extremely high cultural intelligence will encounter specific events and behaviors in a new cultural context that will not be immediately understood. In this case, the leader delays judgment by suspending assumptions and sits with the uncomfortable state of not knowing. CQ strategy includes accepting confusion and maintaining a willingness to not know something, which will lead to a better evaluation of the situation. That, in turn, will lead to eventual, and more accurate, understanding.[7] When we have that kind of understanding and strategy, we're poised for a level of culturally intelligent behavior that offers a competitive edge beyond what typically happens in the management of culturally diverse leaders — simply doing "business as usual." Although my way of getting information about Dr. Jones in Liberia was flawed, the input from my colleague Moses, combined with the intentional time I spent reflecting on the interaction and planning an alternative strategy, moved me beyond my initial impasse. My subsequent conversation was more planned while simultaneously monitoring how the Liberian leader I was questioning responded to my approach and questions. In many regards, it made the difference of whether my trip was a waste of time or actually accomplished one of my primary objectives.

Given the high number of cross-cultural encounters experienced by most of us, it's unrealistic to know precisely what's going on at the deepest level of the iceberg for most of the individuals we encounter. That's a difficult process even with our intimate others. As the only male in my house, I regularly misunderstand what's going on around me with my own family! But at the very least, putting out our antenna to monitor the appropriateness of our assumptions and plan will enhance our cross-cultural performance. Checking helps us confirm or disconfirm whether our interpretations are true and whether our subsequent plans are effective and strategic.

Conclusion

We ended up not partnering with Dr. Jones and Madison College in Monrovia and I recently heard Dr. Harris resigned from his teaching role at the college. I am still, however, using insights I learned from that situation. Currently, I am in the midst of helping an organization for which I'm a board member to develop a partnership with some affiliates in Thailand. We're receiving conflicting counsel about a particular Thai leader and his business. Some advisers say we can't move forward without this leader's involvement. Others caution us against any kind of partnership with him. Doing this kind of due diligence never becomes easy, but CQ strategy is assisting me in developing a plan for how to get the information we need. Thailand and Liberia are vastly different places. But some of the strategies I learned from my work in Liberia can be adapted for this current challenge in Thailand.

Once you learn the skills for CQ strategy, you can apply them to all kinds of relationships and situations. You can even look at a Goth teenager and begin to ask, *What's behind the black clothes, piercings, tattoos, and music?* rather than jump to conclusions about Goth teenagers in general or about that individual. Or you can ask yourself, *What's behind the response I get when I use that same joke in that context as compared to when I use it at the home office?*

CQ strategy is critical for a number of reasons. First, the conscious attempt at awareness promotes active thinking about your work and people in different cultural settings. Second, in planning how to adapt your behavior and work for a different context, CQ strategy invokes creativity and innovation rather than simply relying on the same old practices that seem to work at home. Even after developing a revised strategy for a new cultural context, checking drives us to continually revise and innovate as we monitor the effectiveness of what we're doing.

BEST PRACTICES FOR CQ STRATEGY

1. *Practice the "Why? Why? Why?" strategy*—By repeatedly asking ourselves, "Why?" (five times is a good rule of thumb), we get to the deeper levels of an issue.[8] It might look something like this:

   - We still don't have a contract from Japan. Ask yourself, *Why?*
   - They wouldn't sign it before we left. *Why?*
   - They're uncomfortable Susan is no longer managing the account. *Why?*
   - Trust among Japanese leaders takes a long time. *Why?*
   - Because trust is built on relationships, not signed documents. *Why?*

   Developing CQ strategy in yourself and others can be as simple as reenacting the three-year-old's query, "Why? Why? Why?"

2. *Keep a journal of your cross-cultural reflections*—It can be as basic as doing the observation/interpretation exercise. Or document your cross-cultural experiences along with your questions and insights. Go back later and reread what

you wrote. Do this with some of your colleagues and discuss the insights together.[9]

3. *Examine cross-cultural situations in what you see and read*—When reading business magazines, newspapers, or simply watching a movie, observe cross-cultural scenarios and think of a way you would work through this situation. Don't try to resolve it too quickly but practice becoming aware, developing a plan, and then finding ways to check the appropriateness of your plans.

4. *Engage in active planning*—When you take on a new assignment that involves a high level of cross-cultural engagement, think about how your approach will differ from how you would do this assignment with people from your own culture. Find someone to run this by who can offer informed input.

5. *Find cultural guides*—When working extensively with a particular culture, find someone to be your coach. Select guides carefully. Here are some things to look for:

- Can they distinguish what's different about this culture from others?
- Do they demonstrate self-awareness? Other awareness?
- Are they familiar with your culture, including your national culture and your vocational culture (e.g., engineering or health care)?
- Have they worked across numerous cultures themselves?
- Do they ask lots of questions or simply "tell" you.
- Can they articulate what kinds of personalities often get most frustrated in this culture?

A cultural guide with a good measure of multicultural awareness will serve you well. One of the greatest things they can do is help you know what kinds of questions you should ask of yourself and others as you move into this assignment.

CHAPTER 7

RUN, WALK, OR JOG: CQ ACTION (STEP 4)

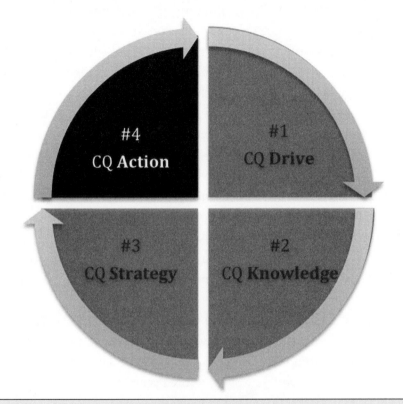

STEP 4: CQ ACTION:	
What behaviors do I need to adjust?	
Changing verbal and nonverbal actions appropriately when interacting cross-culturally	
Profile of a leader with high CQ action:	Leaders with high CQ action can draw on the other three dimensions of CQ to translate their enhanced motivation, understanding, and planning into action. They possess a broad repertoire of behaviors, which they can use depending on the context.

Two years ago, Simon left his role as a CEO of a growing company in Chicago and became president of a small, private liberal arts college in New England. The college has enjoyed a long reputation for offering an excellent liberal arts education but has been at a plateau for the last decade. The organizational structure is inflexible; enrollment is in decline; and the college has very little ethnic diversity among its faculty, staff, and students. Simon and the college seemed like a perfect match. Education is something Simon has always valued, not the least of which is evident by his Ph.D. in business from the University of Chicago. He thrives on coming in and reinventing an organization. He's an innovator, a charismatic leader, and naturally curious about different cultures given his own Chinese-American heritage. I met Simon when he agreed to be part of my research on cultural intelligence among academic leaders. Simon describes himself as obsessive-compulsive. He's extremely fit, his clothes are always neatly pressed, and his office is meticulously tidy. His magnetic smile matches his contagious personality.

Simon described his first two years at the college as the hardest assignment he had ever been given. This was no small statement coming from him. The last company he led filed for bankruptcy just before he arrived. In less than three years, he led a turnaround resulting in the company's most profitable year over its twenty-five-year history. And the business he led prior to that one was also in crisis before he came in and quickly gave it a bright, new future. But Simon felt like he had met his match. There were far too few results from his first twenty-four months of leading the college. Sure, the financial picture was more sound and enrollment had at least held steady. But that was far from the kind of performance Simon was used to.

Simon had a decent understanding of the academic subculture. He knew he couldn't just apply the same kinds of leadership approaches at the college that he used in the business world.

And while the New England community where he was now living had less ethnic diversity than he had ever experienced in his life, he has always been able to adapt to new cultural surroundings. Simon was highly motivated to see the college thrive and he drew on his understanding of business and education to develop a plan for turning around the college's flat numbers. But there was something that kept him from feeling like he was really leading effectively, which was unlike anything he had ever experienced as a leader.

While visiting Simon at his college, he invited me to sit in on a personnel meeting where he was giving an update and casting a vision for the future. Just a few minutes into Simon's presentation, I was captivated. His content was substantive, he offered some humor, and he communicated an inspiring vision for the college. I was almost ready to ask him for a job! After reminding myself why I was there, I looked around and began to wonder why there were so many blank stares. The faculty and staff couldn't have looked more bored and disengaged. If I had been speaking, their glassy eyes would have sucked the life out of me. But Simon kept at it. If anything, his charisma and delivery seemed to become more electric the longer he went on.

Being motivated to run at a challenge like the one facing Simon is really important. And having knowledge about the various cultures where you lead is essential, including the organizational culture and the various national and ethnic cultures represented. Then, being able to draw on that understanding to interpret and plan is essential. But at the end of the day, the question is, can I effectively lead in this context? Can I bring about the necessary results? Our individual leadership is ultimately judged based on whether or not we bring about results.

The final step toward cultural intelligence, CQ action, is where the rubber meets the road. Do we know what someone is talking about? Are we able to communicate effectively? Can we lead people respectfully and adjust our behavior as needed while still remaining true to who we are? CQ action is the extent to which we *appropriately* change our verbal and nonverbal actions when we interact cross-culturally. The goal is to be yourself while figuring out which behaviors need to change in order to accomplish your objectives. As noted at the beginning of this book, one of the revolutionary aspects of the cultural intelligence model is the emphasis on inward transformation in our perspective and outlook rather than just trying to master the "dos" and avoid the taboos. Artificial attempts to modify behavior invite inflexibility and fall short of giving us a sustainable approach to leading cross-culturally.[1] The degree to which we continue to change internally will be seen in the impressions we leave on others through our actions.

Ironically, the most effective way to manipulate our behavior is through the other three steps of the CQ cycle. CQ action is primarily the outcome of our drive, knowledge, and strategy. In one sense, this whole book is about CQ action because our behavior is really the only way someone will know whether we're culturally intelligent. With that in mind, it's important to emphasize a few specific behaviors to adapt. The three subdimensions of CQ action are *verbal behavior, nonverbal behavior,* and *speech acts.*[2] These sub-dimensions inform the ways we can develop our capabilities in CQ action. CQ action can be enhanced by adapting our communication, learning to negotiate differently, and knowing when to flex and when not to flex.

HOW TO DEVELOP CQ ACTION

Adapt your communication.

Negotiate differently.

Know when to flex and when not to flex.

Key question: What behaviors should I adapt for this cross-cultural assignment?

Adapt Your Communication

In describing ways to develop CQ knowledge, we noted the importance of understanding language and its role in effective leadership. (See Chapter 5.) Whether casting vision, building trust, giving directions, or addressing conflict, it all centers around whether we can get the message across. Nearly every book on leadership includes a section on the importance of communication. For me, Simon's communication was lucid and compelling. But it appeared his personnel didn't receive it the same way I did. At least that's what I observed. I needed to find out if I was accurately interpreting what I perceived. In fact, as I interviewed some of the faculty and staff, I found that indeed they weren't nearly as inspired by Simon's vision casting as I was. The recurring responses from faculty when asked to describe Simon's leadership was that he was an outsider who was trying to turn the college into a business. Several professors were unnerved by the way Simon continually used words like *bottom-line, enterprise,* and *capitalize.* This was proof to them that Simon didn't understand the academic world. And given that he often referenced stories from his corporate background and frequently cited the University of Phoenix as a success story, his impassioned, articulate presentations had little impact on them.[3] Some of the college staff had similar responses but a more common theme in their feedback was the inauthenticity they perceived from Simon's constant enthusiasm. Most of the staff members at the college were native to New England and listening to a public speaker with so much energy and charisma caused them to feel like Simon was trying to sell them something. They couldn't get beyond the sense that his delivery made them feel like he was performing rather than just talking with them as colleagues. One woman even characterized him as a "used car salesman," a derogatory slur to suggest Simon was trying to swindle and manipulate the collegiate community. The cultural realities of this New England college were in conflict with the ways Simon had always communicated as a leader. We often miss the cultural differences that exist right within our own borders.

Leaders communicate all day long—making presentations, writing e-mail, talking on the phone, sitting in meetings, and informally going about their work. Like so many of these leadership tasks, the challenge of effective communication is heightened when trying to communicate with individuals across different cultural contexts, whether those differences are ethnic, regional, or organizational. No one at Simon's college referenced his Asian background as a roadblock. But his corporate, Midwest background seemed to be a huge roadblock for them.

The ability to communicate effectively in a new cultural context is a prime example of how CQ action becomes the natural outgrowth of the other three CQ steps. There's a level of motivation and energy (CQ drive) needed to relearn how to communicate in ways that build trust and motivate people in a new context. There's a great deal of understanding (CQ knowledge) needed to know what cultural systems and values are utilized and the words to use and avoid. And a heightened level of awareness, planning, and checking (CQ strategy) is necessary to actually communicate the relevant ideas and images. In drawing on these other steps toward CQ, there are three kinds of communication behaviors that most need our attention: *words*, *delivery*, and *nonverbal actions*.[4]

Words

Words allow us to exchange ideas, communicate trust, and negotiate toward win-win situations. The very words that create vision and expectation in one cultural context can be the same ones that instill distrust and suspicion in another. I can think of several people from many contexts who would have listened to Simon's presentation and found it inspiring and right on the mark. But that's not how it was received by his college personnel. It doesn't really matter if I was inspired by Simon. His team wasn't!

There are a few different ways to think about how we use words when we lead cross-culturally: topics, orders and requests, apologies, and compliments.

TOPICS

Appropriately adapting our behavior involves learning what topics of discussion are appropriate in various settings. Although this applies to work-related conversations, it's most apparent in more informal, social interactions. For example, the after-hours drink with someone from a different cultural background is often far more challenging than interactions revolving around work. Yet, these informal interactions are often the more important ones.

Sometimes people from other cultures have asked me how much money I make or how much my home costs, questions that would be considered off limits even among close friends in my context. And I've been with colleagues who have been told they're looking very "fat," a description I teach my kids to never use in reference to anyone. But these topics might not be considered disrespectful at all in other cultures. In fact, being told you're "fat" in many African cultures is a real compliment. It's evidence you're wealthy and successful. Other times I've been the one who has come across as rude. I've asked single friends from other cultures about their love lives only to learn I'm being too forward according to their cultural norms. Or I've neglected to ask about their families or share more about mine.

There are many other examples. Religion and politics are typically seen as off-limits topics among American colleagues unless there's a clear invitation to go there. But many German individuals value overt expressions of opinion on these kinds of topics in order to have a good argumentative exchange. For many Germans, getting to know someone means finding out what the other person's positions are on different issues and debating them as a means of interaction. In contrast, when Chinese individuals meet for the first time, their approach for getting to know each other is usually quite different. Instead of heated dialogue and debating each other, you usually start by talking about your family background and asking others about theirs. Only after that kind of rapport is developed is it appropriate to discuss social and political issues. Americans and Japanese often talk about business long into the dinner hour, but British individuals tend to think shoptalk needs to stop once the workday is over. Different conventions for selecting conversational strategies and topics are an area of behavior we may need to adapt.[5]

Few things demonstrate the cultural variance of conversational topics more than humor. Jokes and things we find funny often depend on an assumed understanding and history. I was recently on a flight sitting next to a Chinese-American businesswoman. She often travels to China to translate for English-speaking corporate trainers who conduct seminars there. She commented on how most of the American and British trainers with whom she works start their presentations with a joke or humorous anecdote. This is an approach that seems to work well for them in their own context. But my seatmate told me that when they do that in China, instead of translating what they're saying, she says to the Mandarin-speaking audience, "Our presenter is telling a joke right now. The polite thing to do will be to laugh when he's done." Humor is deeply rooted in cultural assumptions.

Culturally intelligent leaders understand that the topics we talk about, particularly in social, informal settings, are embedded in cultural values and assumptions that can only be understood with CQ strategy that looks beneath the surface. Discernment in how to use words begins with considering appropriate topics for conversation.

ORDERS AND REQUESTS

Helen Spencer-Oatey, a renowned linguistic researcher, describes the cultural variances related to giving orders. In a culture like China's, where communication tends to happen very indirectly, the power of suggestion will be used to make a request. However, in a culture like that of the United States, orders and requests will be much more direct. Think about the progression from a very direct to a very indirect approach to ask an employee to run a budget report:

- "Run the budget report!"
- "I want you to run the budget report."
- "How about running the budget report?"
- "Can you run the budget report?"
- "Wouldn't it help to have a budget report?"[6]

Leaders have to learn the level of comfort individuals and cultures have with direct versus indirect orders and requests and adjust accordingly. There's further variance in how this communication practice relates to a culture's value of power distance. The same culture that values indirect communication may also be a place where senior leaders give explicit and direct commands to subordinates if there's a high level of power distance. But a subordinate would be expected to use extremely indirect communication to make a request of a superior. Peers are expected to use indirect communication with one another lest it seem one is taking on an authoritative role over the other. You need to learn where you're perceived in the hierarchical structure to gage the appropriate level of directness to employ.

Suzanne, an American expatriate working in France, discovered the importance of how she framed a request when she'd go shopping in Paris. Suzanne was fluent in French but that didn't mitigate the challenges she felt in communicating. Early on during her sojourn in France, she couldn't seem to get beyond her perception that French people disliked Americans in general. Whenever she asked for something specific of a shopkeeper, such as, "Where can I find the lipstick?" she received a curt response. One day, a French friend suggested, "Try starting with something like this when you walk into the store: 'Could you help me with a problem?' And if they say 'Yes'—which they more than likely will—then ask for help finding the lipstick." Suzanne tried it and couldn't believe how it seemed to change the disposition of the people waiting on her compared with her previous approach. She was now posturing herself as someone in need rather than coming in and making demands. She began to apply the same kind of strategy with her colleagues and subordinates at work. She was amazed how this simple adjustment altered the way her requests were received. Simply understanding some basic shifts in language can make all the difference in achieving our objectives, whether it's to purchase lipstick or to launch a full-orbed initiative.[7] The most important phrase I try to learn in the language spoken anyplace I visit is "I'm sorry, I don't speak _____. Do you speak English?" It postures me as being in need rather than presuming everyone would be happy to help in English.

APOLOGIES

Another communication challenge is knowing when and how to apologize. People in most cultures would agree that an apology of some sort is needed when an offense occurs. The question is, what's considered offensive and what's the most appropriate way to express regret for an offense?

I've often said, "Sorry! Sorry!" for bumping into people in places like Brazil only to have them look at me as if to say, *Sorry for what?!* To invade one's personal space is a violation in my culture but close proximity and sharing personal space is a part of life for many Brazilians. It's important to learn if and how to apologize to a culturally different colleague when offending that person. For example, an individual coming from an event-time culture might see little offense in being an hour late to a meeting but a culturally intelligent individual will understand that keeping someone from a clock-time culture waiting for an hour requires an apology. In the mind of most people from clock-time cultures, to be kept waiting for an hour is to have wasted their time and disrespects them. And in cultures where hierarchy is important, a lower-status individual is expected to offer great deference and an apologetic posture to someone with higher status, even if no great offense has occurred. An outsider need not mimic all these behaviors, something we'll address later in the chapter; but we're wise to understand the importance of these kinds of communication practices.

Korean advertising through e-mail often begins with the sentence, "I am sorry to send you spam." A spam message with an apology is deemed more credible in the Korean context but would be seen as a position of weakness in an American one. Learn when and how to apologize to the people in the cultures with which you regularly work.

In 2001, a U.S. surveillance plane and a Chinese jet fighter collided over the South China Sea. The next several days resulted in heated arguments between U.S. and Chinese diplomats over whether the U.S. Government should apologize. The Chinese Ministry of Foreign Affairs insisted on full responsibility from the U.S. Government. Viewing the aggressiveness of the Chinese fighter jet as the reason for the collision, U.S. Secretary of State Colin Powell refused to issue an apology. His response aligned with the typical U.S. view of apologies. An apology is rooted in a pragmatic understanding of who is at fault. The emphasis of an apology is in looking for responsibility for something done. The Chinese view is oriented around harmony and a bigger view of the circumstances. The emphasis is on a willingness to acknowledge the unfortunate event rather than precisely who was at fault. The Chinese were angered not so much by the incident of a U.S. plane being in their air-space but in the unwillingness to issue an apology.[8] As we become more aware of cultural values (individualism versus collectivism, or clock time versus event time), CQ strategy gives us the ability to translate that understanding into appropriate ways to give and receive apologies.

COMPLIMENTS

The giving and receiving of compliments is another communication exercise that requires cultural intelligence. When complimented, should I receive the compliment or is it better to reject it to avoid seeming self-congratulatory? And when wanting to encourage a colleague or subordinate, is it best to do so publicly or privately? Is a compliment best expressed through words, gifts, or another approach? In many Western cultures, it's largely agreed that the best way to respond to a compliment is to receive it. However, the reverse is true in many Eastern cultures. Rejection or denial of a compliment is deemed more appropriate in places like Japan and China. Of course, this is another example where there are plenty of individual differences among people who share a culture depending on their personality and family upbringing, hence the need for awareness, planning, and checking (CQ strategy) as we compliment and affirm individuals.

A leader might presume a compliment will motivate a subordinate to continue doing good work, but if the individual feels a boss is being too personal and reflecting more intimacy in their relationship than appropriate, it might actually play a demotivating role. And leaders from individualist cultures often single out high-performing staff members and publicly acknowledge them. But that can bring about all kinds of embarrassment and shame for someone in a collectivist culture. On the other hand, leaders in collectivist cultures who offer little personalized affirmation and encouragement to colleagues and clients from individualist cultures can be seen as ungrateful. When I've taught in Singapore, I've often been very uncertain about my effectiveness because of the absence of much personal feedback.

A leader can't expect to master all the norms for appropriate compliments for every cultural encounter. But we're advised to understand and practice some basic adaptive behavior in how we offer encouragement and praise to people from different cultural backgrounds. An overall posture of respect and suspended judgment will help us grow in knowing the appropriate way to communicate gratitude and affirm success.

A great deal of our cross-cultural behavior depends on exchanging words. The greatest challenge exists when different languages are spoken in the same work environment. Leaders are needed who will learn new languages or learn to use translators. But any time we communicate cross-culturally, even when there's a shared language, some basic communication behaviors will play a strong role in how we lead.

Delivery

As important as words are, it wasn't only Simon's words that made the faculty and staff at his college uncomfortable. It was also the way he delivered them. Even when appropriate words are chosen, a great deal of miscommunication can occur in how information is delivered. Culturally intelligent leaders will learn what communication is best offered in writing, when to pick up the phone, and when to communicate face-to-face. They will gain confidence in knowing the appropriate level of enthusiasm, pace, and style to use when talking to different audiences. While leaders in low-power-distance cultures can use the same style of communication when interacting with an administrative assistant as with a vice president, that isn't so in high-power-distance cultures. We'll explore several of the nonverbal dimensions of communication separately in just a minute, but it's important to specifically address the manner in which words are spoken, something often described as "delivery."

Many native-English speakers fail to alter their delivery when communicating with individuals for whom English is a second language. Admittedly, my own style as a public speaker is fast-paced and energetic. I have to continually work on slowing down, especially when speaking publicly to an audience that includes participants for whom English isn't their first language. Here are several strategies for enhancing communication when addressing an audience of second-language English speakers:

- Slow down. Slow down. Slow down.
- Use clear, slow speech. Enunciate carefully.
- Avoid colloquial expressions.
- Repeat important points using different words to explain the same thing.
- Avoid long, compound sentences.
- Use visual representations (pictures, tables, graphs, etc.) to support what is being said.
- Mix presentations with a balance of story and principles.
- Hand out written summaries.
- Pause more frequently.

Most of these same strategies apply to small group and one-on-one communication, too. We have to find the delivery style most comfortable to us so it appears natural and authentic. But we also have to learn what kinds of alterations to make to our natural style when addressing various audiences. Simon needed to find a way to use the public speaking style most comfortable to him while also adjusting for the New England, academic subculture where he was leading. Then, as we learn to alter our delivery, we have to continually check for understanding. It's not enough to simply ask, "Are you with me? Does this make sense?" Instead, we have to create questions and activities that will reveal the level of understanding among those listening.

Nonverbals

It's often been said, "You cannot *not* communicate." Although words and delivery are an important part of the communication exchange, just as much—and possibly more—gets communicated through other nonverbal behaviors. It's important to note a few of the ways culture affects nonverbal behavior, including distance, touching, body position, gestures, facial expressions, and eye contact.

DISTANCE

Most of us have felt the discomfort that comes from someone violating our personal space as we interact. Culture plays a huge role in what we view as appropriate distance. The amount of space between seats when conducting a training session, the way an office is set up, and the way a boss interacts with staff are all ways distance influences the ways we behave cross-culturally. Be alert to how social distance affects your interactions and be prepared to modify it.[9]

TOUCHING

The handshake, although most widely used in Western contexts, has been broadly accepted in professional settings around the world as an appropriate greeting. But the degree of firmness, the appropriate duration for the contact, and the individual who initiates it varies widely from one cultural context to another. Putting a hand on one's back or shoulder is also a form of touching often used in some professional settings. Knowing the appropriate touch for different levels of authority, gender, and age are all important considerations for how we lead. For example, individuals from many high-power-distance cultures have expectations about how handshakes should occur between individuals according to their status. When greeting someone with higher status, individuals are expected to support their wrist with their left hand. Many African cultures use a more gentle handshake than is commonly used in Europe or the United States but linger while holding the other's hand. These cues are important for leading in and out of lots of places. Pay attention to this when observing others as well as in your own interactions. It's generally agreed that the lowest touch cultures are North America, Northern Europe, and Asia. High-touch cultures are those found in Latin America, Southern and Eastern Europe, and the Middle East. As always, beware of individual differences that exist among people in various contexts.

BODY POSITION

There are also unwritten, often even unconscious cultural rules that govern the degree to which individuals sit, stand, and bow. In some contexts, one's gender, age, and level of authority determine where they should position themselves in relation to others. And bowing is a key nonverbal behavior used in many contexts like Japan, Korea, and Thailand. The unwritten rules about bowing in places like these are complex and very difficult for an outsider to master. Rather than becoming overwhelmed, the culturally intelligent leader knows that some of these body positions, such as the bowing rituals in Japan, are best reserved for native Japanese. But we're wise to consider which of our postures should be altered.

GESTURES

People often use gestures to accompany things they're saying. So it's especially difficult to understand gestures if you can't understand the language. And gestures are one of the most highly individualized forms of communication. So while there are some cultural norms, CQ strategy is needed to discern whether the gesture is a reflection of a culture or of an individual. Watch for cues. It's very hard to understand gestures but notice how people point, if they point at all. Continue to observe it in others from the same cultural context. I've inadvertently used what I thought was the "okay" sign in my culture only to have made a profane symbol to an entire audience in Brazil. Test your assumptions and be very cautious before enacting new gestures just because you've observed them in others.

FACIAL EXPRESSION

Most of our cultures teach us how to disguise our emotions when necessary so strangers can't discern how we're really feeling. Sometimes we can see through those expressions, especially when we're in a familiar culture and even more so when it's someone with whom we're in a close relationship. But facial expressions can be highly misleading. This is what happened when the international volunteers I referenced earlier assumed smiling faces by poor people meant they were content with their economic poverty. On the other hand, I've often heard Westerners ask why no one in the photo of an Indian family appears to be smiling. Accurately understanding the meaning behind an individual's facial expressions is one of the most subjective challenges we'll encounter. Exercise extreme caution in making judgments about what a facial expression means when observed cross-culturally.

EYE CONTACT

The other important nonverbal behavior to adapt is eye contact. Different cultures have various norms about when and how long eye contact is appropriate. This becomes further complicated because most cultures have unwritten rules about how to use eye contact according to gender, age, and status. The other day I talked to a manager who said everything about a job candidate suggested she should hire him. But he wouldn't look her in the eye, which made her distrust him. I asked her what his cultural background was. "He's Saudi," she said. Although Arabs often have conventions of longer eye contact, many Saudi men have been socialized all their lives to avoid direct eye contact with women. Most Arabs, Latinos, Indians, and Pakistanis all have conventions of longer eye contact, whereas Africans and East Asians interpret eye contact as conveying anger or insubordination and avoid it.[10]

Even the seasoned traveler with high cultural intelligence can't be expected to master all the communication behaviors used in each culture encountered. As you know by now, the goal isn't to become an expert on the perfect word, delivery, and nonverbal behavior for every situation. Instead, the key is to develop the ability to observe the behavior of others, reflect on it, and learn when to modify our own actions in response. CQ strategy is the best tool for helping us with this process. Regularly review this overview of communication behaviors to refresh your memory on the various differences you're likely to encounter.

Negotiate Differently

Another core behavior for any leader is the ability to effectively negotiate. Regardless of the cultural context, the objective in negotiation is for people to reach an agreement that mutually satisfies their respective interests, both personally and organizationally. Effective negotiations usually include offers and counteroffers with concessions and compromises along the way in order to reach an agreement. Cross-cultural negotiation is another example of how CQ action is the outgrowth of the other three dimensions of CQ. Cross-cultural negotiation takes a great deal of CQ drive, requiring not only the motivation to do what's best for our own organization and interests but also to consider what's best for the interests of the other parties. Effective negotiating also depends on CQ knowledge. We have to gain the necessary understanding to anticipate where the key differences may lie in the cultural systems and values involved. This understanding will enable us to use CQ strategy to develop a thoughtful plan for how to go about the negotiation process in a particular context.[11] There are four specific behaviors useful for cross-cultural negotiation: altering your timing, adapting your style, remaining flexible, and acting with integrity.

Alter Your Timing

One of the primary ways we may need to adapt our negotiation strategies stems from differing expectations regarding the amount of relationship and time required for a signed contract. This is the most consistent theme running through the research done on cross-cultural negotiation and it's similar to differences pointed out earlier.[12] In many Asian and Latino cultures, it's impossible to conceive of reaching an agreement apart from lots of time to get to know each other. Building relationships requires that negotiators take time to get to know one another—eating, drinking, visiting national landmarks, playing golf, or going to a cricket game. This type of ritual socializing is vital because it represents an honest effort to understand as fully as possible the needs, values, and interests of the other side. In contrast, many Western European and North American cultures value expediency in reaching a contractual agreement. For these individuals, vast amounts of time socializing can seem like a disregard for the value of one's time. Culturally intelligent Americans and Germans might need to learn to be sociable and patient when negotiating with people from Japan and Mexico. And culturally intelligent Asians and Latinos might need to learn to get to the point a little more quickly when dealing with people from time-oriented cultures.[13] Adapt your negotiation behavior in light of the various values present with a readiness to further adapt along the way.

In a similar way, good cross-cultural negotiation includes being sensitive to the right timing. McDonald's took nearly a decade to negotiate with Russian leaders in Moscow before selling burgers there. Taking the long view is essential because it's usually going to take longer to negotiate internationally. Allow for that. And learn what times of year are best. Different places shut down at different seasons throughout the year. Adjust your expectations and approach for the amount of time and relationships required to negotiate.

Adapt Your Style

Most leaders coming from individualist cultures have learned to negotiate aggressively and assertively. While looking for a win-win situation, working for your own interests is expected in many Western contexts. Assertive, strong tactics are viewed as strengths in most North American business dealings. But these leaders need to adapt that posture when negotiating in more collectivist cultures in order to attend to the high value placed on cooperation and harmony.[14] Similarly, individuals from assertive cultures like the United States, Nigeria, and India have to make a conscious effort to talk less and listen more when in the midst of negotiations abroad. Active listening will communicate respect and make you a more informed negotiator. Ask open-ended questions and be fully present rather than just asking questions to put on a pretense of interest. As you listen and negotiate, be aware of an overreliance on cultural stereotypes. They're a good first guess. But as we've been continually reminded, too quickly generalizing cultural values to every individual or organization in a culture is dangerous. We have to use the awareness of CQ strategy to get below the surface of the iceberg and attend to the specific individuals and organization involved. Simultaneously, we need to remain alert to how we're being viewed. What kind of preconceptions do the other individuals have given our cultural background or previous experiences? How will we need to compensate for those perceptions?

Remain Flexible

Once we have a negotiation plan in mind, we have to hold it loosely and be ready to flex. We're never fully in control of what happens but especially when it involves cross-cultural collaboration. Be prepared for the unexpected and develop adaptive skills. Anticipate where you should be willing to determine your nonnegotiables. You don't want to make concessions you'll later regret, but you also don't want to lose the deal because of inflexibility. In the midst of the negotiation, draw on the skills developed in CQ strategy to stay alert to what's going on behind the scenes in the negotiating process. Be ready to abandon your assumptions when things go in a different direction than anticipated. The constant reshaping and adapting required in cross-cultural negotiations is at the core of CQ action.

Act with Integrity

Finally, regardless of the cultural context, there are no shortcuts for building and creating trust. Despite the many cultural differences for how trust gets communicated and built, it rests on ethical principles. Admittedly, there's a great deal of ambiguity about what constitutes ethical practice, particularly across different cultural contexts. But it's imperative we remain true to our own ethical principles and to those of our prospective partner. Avoid shortcuts that result in reduced product safety, abusive labor practices, deceptive advertising, or environmental degradation. Not only will they hurt you ethically but in the long run, they will hurt business as well. Never lose sight of the triple bottom line (see Chapter 3) and always interact with honor and respect. Whether it's fair-trade practices that pay laborers a worthy wage, environmental responsibility that avoids polluting rivers to produce a product, or holding subcontractors accountable for the kinds of labor practices we'd use in our own company, the importance of behaving ethically as we work internationally cannot be overstated.

The negotiation process in a cross-cultural context is the synthesis of all four CQ dimensions. Leaders and organizations with cultural intelligence have an edge in the negotiation process. Be ready to adapt the way you negotiate as you work in various contexts.

Know When to Flex and When Not to Flex

There's one more very important skill to master to enhance CQ action. Should we mimic the behavior of people in other cultures or not? Too much adaptation can generate suspicion and distrust and yet we've continually noted that inflexible behavior is a sure death wish for most twenty-first-century leaders and organizations. When should we alter our strategy and when should it remain unchanged? When is it okay to pass on eating something that turns your stomach, and when should we eat and pray, "Dear God, help me keep it down?" As we broaden our repertoire of cultural understanding and behavior, we'll become more attuned to knowing which response is appropriate.

Learning if and when it's appropriate to adapt our behavior to another culture is a complex question. It's more than just knowing the behavior of people from other cultures. It requires drawing on CQ knowledge and CQ strategy to anticipate what people from other cultures expect of us. Singaporeans have preconceived notions of how they expect Aussies to behave and vice versa. Latin Americans have ideas of how they expect African Americans to behave. The globalization of television, movies, and music has played a huge role in creating preconceived perceptions of people in various cultures. Even if the portrayed norms are inaccurate, the perceptions they leave can still be very real. If you act in ways different from those preconceived expectations, you're wise to think about what that will communicate to your observers. As we engage with individuals from different cultural backgrounds, we should ask ourselves, How do these people expect me to act based on my cultural context? How should that affect my behavior? What misconceptions are likely to be present in their assumptions about me? These are all critical considerations for how we interact and lead.

One of my own learning curves in CQ action has involved the realization that cultural intelligence is a two-way street. One time I came to Singapore directly from Sierra Leone, West Africa. When I got to Singapore, I began venting to my colleague Soon Ang about the group of Americans I observed in Sierra Leone who took their bottled water and antibacterial wash with them everywhere they went. No sooner would they greet people than they'd publicly lather their hands with antibacterial wash. It just seemed incredibly insensitive and obnoxious to me. Soon asked me, "So why do you expect the Americans to stop using their antibacterial wash publicly, but you don't expect the Sierra Leoneans to know Americans are more susceptible to getting sick in places like this?"

I argued the Americans were the ones who went abroad as guests so they couldn't very well demand their hosts adjust to them. At the same time, many of our cross-cultural encounters don't involve clear distinctions of guest and host. So we need to explore ways to make cultural intelligence something we encourage in both directions. Soon's point is well taken. The richest cross-cultural relationships involve culturally intelligent behavior flowing both ways. Some of us may be in leadership roles where we can help foster and develop cultural intelligence on both sides of the border.

This brings us back to the question, to flex or not to flex? I wouldn't advise these Americans to drink the water from the village well. Clearly, travelers need to take realistic precautions for preventing illness against themselves and their families regardless of the potential offense created. But the American guests I observed could have reduced their offense if they had simply been more discreet about how and when they used their antibacterial wash and bottled water.

There *are* some situations where the best option is not to adapt at all. Adjusting to the behavior of the other culture is a double-edged sword. Some level of adapting to communication styles and patterns cross-culturally is usually viewed positively because it leads to perceptions of similarity. However, high levels of adaptation are viewed negatively. Extensive mimicry will be seen as insincere and possibly even deceptive.[15] Individuals who "go native" try to entirely strip themselves of their own culture in a fit of enthusiasm for another culture. These individuals can be seen embracing all the values and practices of a new culture with an eagerness that perplexes even those who are part of that culture. Uncritically accepting everything in a new culture and turning one's back on one's own birth culture is not culturally intelligent behavior.

I've often observed this among adults who work with adolescents. Youth are usually grateful for adult teachers and coaches who try to understand and respect what's behind students' fashions and music. But that doesn't mean they want their teachers to start dressing like them and mirroring their iPod playlists. There's nothing worse than seeing a fifty-year-old coach dress and act like a fifteen-year-old. Likewise, in most places, it's viewed as humorous and downright silly when outsiders try to wear native dress. Women dressing more modestly than they might at home or men dressing up or down more according to the cultural norm is appropriate. But going fully native in our dress isn't usually the way to go. Similarly, if I'm invited to participate at a conference in Japan, most Japanese will be favorably impressed if I am courteous, polite, and somewhat reserved. But they don't expect me to master the intricate social skills of Japan such as bowing in all the appropriate ways. A slight bow or drop of the head is sufficient. In fact, if I try to mimic cultures like these too much, at best my behavior will be seen as amusing, and more likely, it will be seen as offensive.

To flex or not to flex? How do we know? These questions bring home why CQ action is primarily a culmination of the other three steps toward cultural intelligence. Rather than simply mimicking the behaviors we observe, we need to adapt based on the knowledge of the other culture and the expectations of the people. Using that cultural understanding, CQ strategy will help us pay attention to the appropriate cues in order to evaluate the possible outcomes and to know which behavior is appropriate. We have to ask: When will adapting our behavior to that of others enhance the accomplishment of our objectives? When will doing so impede our performance or at the very least seem strained and awkward? The cultures with which we have ongoing, extended contact are settings where we must diligently learn which behaviors to adjust.

With experience and growing levels of cultural intelligence, some of our adaptive behavior may become so well learned that we will adapt naturally without much conscious thought. That's the goal. We want to get to a point where this high level of thinking and action happens as naturally as the thoughts and behaviors enacted in our familiar cultural contexts. But getting there might be as simple as trial and error. Try flexing a bit and see what happens. Test it in lots of different situations. Ask a trusted peer who understands the cultural context how flexing or not flexing will be perceived by others. Then ask someone else. Then ask another person.

Behavior is ambiguous. The same action can have many different meanings depending on who does it, where, and with whom. But by walking through the four-step cycle of CQ, we can better discern which behaviors to adapt and those *not* to adapt.

Conclusion

My two girls are very different from each other. Emily is a homebody who loves to hang out, snuggle together reading a book, and share a long meal together. Grace, on the other hand, is constantly moving. She's happiest when there's a lot going on. She wants to walk to the store, hang out by the lake, throw a Frisbee, or work on an art project all in the same hour. I want to relate to my kids in ways that express my deep love for them. So I interact with them differently according to their unique personalities. I'm not being a chameleon. I simply want them to experience my love in ways that are meaningful to each of them.

We can't possibly learn the individual preferences of all the people we encounter in our work. But learning the cultural norms of different groups of people helps us behave more effectively and respectfully. That's why cultural intelligence is so important to me. It's an essential competency for me as a leader to treat my fellow humanity with dignity and respect. And it allows me to adapt my behavior to accomplish my objectives.

The most common problems in leadership across different cultural contexts are not technical or administrative. The biggest challenges lie in miscommunication, misunderstanding, personality conflicts, poor leadership, and bad teamwork. Cultural intelligence is demonstrated through our social interactions in cross-cultural relationships. The behavioral dimension of cultural intelligence involves learning from our motivation, cultural understanding, and strategies to appropriately adapt our communication and negotiation practices. CQ action is choosing the best actions from a well-developed repertoire of behaviors that are correct for different situations.

We can enjoy and respect the norms and customs of others without thinking we have to conform to everything we observe. The point isn't to accomplish flawless cross-cultural behavior. In fact, some of the greatest lessons to be learned happen in our cultural faux pas. But as we build on our perseverance, understanding, and interpretation, we come closer to behaving in ways that allow for effective leadership.

BEST PRACTICES FOR CQ ACTION

1. *Learn what practices and taboos are most important for the key regions where you work.* Knowing when and how to exchange a business card, the protocols for gift giving, and whether or not to use the left hand are a few of the specific behaviors worth mastering. Although you can't master all the practices and taboos, you can learn which ones will most enhance or deter effectiveness.

2. *Look for consistent feedback.* Encouragement as well as corrective feedback is essential for developing CQ action. Look for ways to get an honest assessment of your work. Both positive and negative feedback is an effective way to enhance your ability to flex your behavior.

3. *Go together.* Whenever you have a meeting or a trip that involves cross-cultural work, bring someone along. Jointly processing the challenges and rewards of cross-cultural negotiation and work is much more effective than doing so individually.

4. *Assess for CQ action in all key management hires.* While hiring an increasingly diverse workforce is a vital and strategic

choice, it's not enough to simply hire more women
and more people of color. Every management position,
even — and especially — positions held by individuals coming from the dominant culture, should be held by people
with culturally intelligent behavior.

5. *Develop a zero-tolerance policy for inappropriate jokes and
language directed toward any specific cultural group (including socioethnic, sexual orientation, and religious). Encourage*
diversity by allowing flexibility in dress and behavior
as long as it doesn't interfere with your organizational
objectives.

Part III

How Do I Apply CQ?

CHAPTER 8

SEE THE JOURNEY AHEAD: PROOF AND
CONSEQUENCES OF CQ

Simon lasted another six months at the New England college before he decided it just wasn't a good fit. He grew significantly in his ability to see what was going on and he was able to articulate some of the behaviors he would need to change to adapt to the school's culture. However, he didn't perceive a mutual willingness to adapt to him.

As if the challenge of leading a struggling school in New England wasn't enough, Simon went on to acquire a fledgling company that provides executive coaching and training to senior leaders. The company had been very successful in the United States, but the last owner expanded the business into Europe and Asia and the profit margins had been in decline for the last five years. Last year the company lost one million dollars. Simon learned some key things about himself and the challenge of leading in various cultures—organizational, regional, and ethnic. He wanted to see if he could run at a new multicultural challenge and help other leaders do the same. Over the next several months, Simon and I exchanged dozens of e-mails and phone calls, and we shared a few meals together. He wanted to learn more about cultural intelligence to see if he could apply it to his own leadership and to the leadership of those his company served.

In his direct but affable way, he said to me, "Okay, Dave! Show me what the CQ research means for people like me." He had three primary questions for me:

1. "Are there any proven results from leading with cultural intelligence?"

2. "Is there any way to predict whether someone has cultural intelligence?"

3. "What are the best ways to develop cultural intelligence?"

This chapter began as a conversation with Simon. First, I summarized for him the consequences of leading with CQ, next I shared things that can predict someone's CQ, and finally I reviewed dozens of ways to become more culturally intelligent. In a similar fashion, the first two sections of this chapter offer a brief summary of the research findings about key results and predictors of cultural intelligence.[1] The "Ways to Develop CQ" section later in this chapter lists several practical suggestions for developing CQ.

Results of CQ

We come back full circle to the question in Chapter 1: Why CQ? Now that we have a fuller understanding of what CQ is and how to develop it, so what? A growing number of executives identify CQ as being highly instrumental in offering them a competitive advantage for tapping into the opportunities of the twenty-first-century landscape. The research demonstrates that organizations and leaders who prioritize cultural intelligence are more likely to accomplish their mission. In fact, evidence is mounting that organizations that prioritize cultural intelligence are experiencing several benefits, including the following:

Enhanced Performance

CQ is a strong predictor of a leader's overall performance and adjustment when placed in multicultural situations.[2] In fact, when tested among executives across several organizations around the world, the relationship between CQ and a leader's successful performance cross-culturally was much stronger than the relationship between a leader's demographic characteristics (age, gender, location) and how he or she performs in multicultural contexts. The same was true of general cognitive abilities. CQ was more strongly related to an individual's overall performance cross-culturally than things like academic achievement or an exceptional IQ. In particular, CQ drive, CQ strategy, and CQ action are found to have a positive relationship on an individual's success in accomplishing a task.[3]

Barclays, a mammoth financial services provider, utilized cultural intelligence with top leaders to deal with the company's burgeoning operations across Europe, Africa, Asia, Australia, the Americas, and the Middle East. As the company began to weave cultural intelligence throughout the top levels of the company, Barclays experienced growth in the level of local ownership felt across its widespread global workforce. Lloyds TSB took the challenge of improving customer relationships through CQ, which resulted in increased income streams and better cost management. And Levi Strauss has significantly altered its global marketing strategy as a result of CQ and simultaneously found a correlation in the company's profit margins.[4] Many other businesses, universities, charitable organizations, and governments have seen similar positive gains from using cultural intelligence to achieve their desired outcomes.

Better Decision Making

The commonsense, lead-with-your-gut approach to making decisions doesn't cut it in the twenty-first-century world. As noted in Chapter 1, the biggest challenge identified by today's senior-level executives is understanding customers across multiple locations.[5] As overseas markets become more important, leaders across a wide range of organizations acknowledge a positive relationship between cultural intelligence and their ability to make informed decisions in light of the endless cultural differences.

Without the understanding offered by cultural intelligence, organizations are at a disadvantage for making strategic decisions both in their day-to-day operations and particularly in the midst of a crisis.[6] No industry has felt the need for better judgment across cross-cultural situations than the airlines. Since 9/11, airlines are more acutely aware of the potential of having to handle a crisis. Pilots from two or even three different cultural backgrounds commonly share cockpits and flying responsibilities. International flights depend on communication between pilots and air traffic controllers across numerous countries. We all want these individuals to be able to effectively communicate and make good decisions. Lufthansa Airlines believes cultural intelligence plays a central part in its overall crisis management strategy. Cultural intelligence has been found to predict better decision making from leaders who are working with cross-cultural issues and people (almost all of us!). In particular, there is a positive relationship between the dimensions of CQ knowledge and CQ strategy with better decision making.[7]

Flexibility

Flexibility is the ability most often cited as a necessity for working across cultures. But rarely are leaders offered specific training and skills in how to become more flexible. Cultural intelligence is positively related to a leader's ability to work and adapt in an environment where the assumptions, values, and traditions differ from those in the local context.[8]

Divisional managers and CEOs with higher levels of CQ work more effectively with multicultural teams than do leaders with lower levels of CQ.[9] They have more success in forming collaborative environments across a diversity of cultures and they can adapt their strategies for use in different cultural situations.

International Expansion

Cultural intelligence also plays a significant role in a leader's ability to develop and expand internationally. Doug Flint, CFO of banking giant HSBC, says,

> If you were to go into any business forum in Europe and America and ask which country is going to be most important in the global environment in the next twenty-five years, I suspect that a vast majority would say China, and the second-highest number might say India. If you then ask how much do people in Europe and America understand about the history and culture of those countries, the answer would be a negligible amount.[10]

Organizations with culturally intelligent leaders at the highest levels of management are more likely to succeed in expanding into offshore markets than those with leaders with lower levels of cultural intelligence. Everything from mastering the ability to negotiate and lobby with various governments to effectively utilizing informal channels of communication are skills that are more likely among leaders who are culturally intelligent.[11]

Employer of Choice

In Chapter 1, we noted attracting and retaining good talent is another pressing need felt by leading executives.[12] A company's chances of being the employer of choice is enhanced when recruits see CQ valued and modeled throughout the organization as a whole. Companies like Novartis and Nike found their sharpest recruits identified a culturally intelligent mind-set as one of the most important things they sought in a potential employer. They wanted to join companies like IBM who see diversity as a leading growth edge for business rather than seeing it as a roadblock or a necessary evil.

About 85 percent of emerging leaders "strongly agree" that global sensibilities and a commitment to the common good are extremely important to them in thinking about a current or future employer. They want places of employment where they can grow and develop in CQ by seeing it modeled and prioritized.[13]

Prevention of Burnout and Creation of Personal Satisfaction

Leaders who develop cultural intelligence are less likely to experience burnout, a major threat to today's organizations and leaders. This finding was especially true for short-term business travelers who are expected to fly in and out of lots of different places from month to month.[14] With cultural intelligence, these travelers have a four-step model to guide them. Stress and fatigue are inevitable outcomes for any leader working in increasingly diverse contexts. It's harder work to do the same tasks in a new culture than when done at home. Cultural intelligence mitigates the burnout that often ensues from leading through cross-cultural situations and as a result, it creates an enhanced sense of personal satisfaction. It's related to the development of transformational leadership skills.[15]

Much more research is needed to further validate the results of leading with cultural intelligence; however, the initial results are extremely promising. Simon agreed. Just one year into acquiring his new business, Simon had made the executive coaching company profitable again. Although the international expansion created a loss in previous years at the company, the global markets yielded the greatest returns under Simon's first year of leadership.

Predictors of CQ

What, if anything, predicts whether someone has cultural intelligence? Dozens of studies have been conducted across the Americas,

Asia, Australia, and Europe to investigate what personality traits and experiences are likely to influence an individual toward enhanced CQ. These are important findings to aid in the hiring and promotion process.

Personality Traits

When defining cultural intelligence in Chapter 2, it was noted that the emphasis of cultural intelligence is *not* about one's predisposed personality but on a capability that can be developed. Anyone can grow in cultural intelligence. Having said that, there are some connections between the Big Five personality traits and the four dimensions of cultural intelligence. The Big Five model of personality traits is considered to be the most comprehensive data-driven enquiry into personality. Note the overview in Table 8-1 of how these five personality traits are related to the dimensions of CQ. An *X* signifies a positive relationship between the personality trait and the respective dimension of CQ (e.g., "Extroversion" predicts higher levels of CQ drive, CQ knowledge, and CQ behavior, but not CQ strategy. "Agreeableness" predicts higher levels of CQ action but not the other three dimensions).[16]

If you do an Internet search for Big Five personality tests, several free online tests provide an instant self-report on your tendencies in each of these traits. This kind of understanding can help you see which CQ dimensions might come more naturally to you than others. Being an extrovert is not a sure predictor of having higher CQ action. But when joined with the other ways to develop CQ, there is a positive relationship between extraversion and CQ action. As noted in Table 8-1, an openness to experiences, or a curiosity about the world, is positively related to all four dimensions of CQ. Explore the relevance of the other relationships identified in Table 8-1 for you and your team.

Table 8-1. Relationship Between Personality Traits and Cultural Intelligence

Personality Trait	Definition	Drive	Knowledge	Strategy	Action
Extroversion	The degree to which an individual is outgoing, social, and derives energy from being with people	X	X		X
Agreeableness	The degree to which an individual is cooperative and trusting rather than suspicious and antagonistic				X
Conscientiousness	The degree to which an individual is disciplined and planned more than spontaneous			X	
Emotional Stability	The degree to which one is emotionally steady with limited anxiety				X
Openness to Experience	The degree to which one is imaginative and open to varying experiences and perspectives	X	X	X	X

Experiences

There are also three key experiences that consistently reveal a positive relationship with CQ: cross-cultural experience, educational level, and working in multicultural teams. These experiences informed several of the best practices suggested throughout the book for enhancing cultural intelligence.

Cross-cultural experience by itself does not ensure cultural intelligence, but when wed with the other capabilities of cultural intelligence, it plays a significant role. In particular, individuals with multiple experiences in a variety of places experience more of the benefits of cross-cultural interactions and travel than those who have been in only one or two places, even if for a long time. At the same time, the more countries where you've lived for more than a year, the more positive connection there is between your cross-cultural experience and cultural intelligence.[17] Childhood experiences play less of a role in developing CQ than do adult experiences where we make our own choices about our cross-cultural travel, work, and interaction. On the whole, cross-cultural experience is positively related to all four dimensions of CQ and to one's overall CQ abilities. The growing worldwide travel occurring among many individuals is a promising influence for growing cultural intelligence.[18]

One's educational level is also positively related to cultural intelligence. Advanced training, both formal and informal, shows a positive relationship with one's overall cultural intelligence score. University-level and postgraduate education, in particular, nurture an ability to critically engage with more complex ways of perceiving the world. Again, although not a sole predictor, education level and cultural intelligence are positively related.[19] Although training shouldn't be the only way we develop CQ, it is valuable.

Finally, our global identity is our sense of belonging to culturally diverse work teams. The degree to which you've participated in multicultural teams plays a role in helping you adapt to various cultural situations. There's a positive relationship between cultural intelligence and working for an organization with a diverse team rather than a homogeneous one.[20]

There are a number of other relationships being researched including the influence of gender, age, religious orientation, and profession on CQ; but the research on these factors is still too incomplete to suggest any predictive relationships. Although seeing the connection between these personality traits and experiences can be helpful, cultural intelligence is dynamic and it's a set of abilities that can be nurtured and grown in all of us, regardless of our personality traits and experiences. The most helpful way to assess CQ in ourselves and others is through a CQ assessment and by looking for the indicators described throughout Chapters 3 to 7.

Ways to Develop CQ

Finally, we need to explore concrete ways to develop cultural intelligence as we go about our busy lives. Part II of the book was devoted to describing how to develop CQ through the four-step cycle, a summary of which appears in the summary chart on page 176. In addition, there are dozens of practical ways to tap into everyday activities to grow in cultural intelligence. Some of these ideas appeared previously in the best practices for each step, but I've included a one-stop list here for some really simple ways to work on developing cultural intelligence.

- *Read.* A book like this one can offer a quick introduction to a concept like cultural intelligence but biographies, memoirs, and novels offer a much more robust, visceral encounter with cross-cultural people and places. Check out my suggestions at www.davidlivermore.com.
- *Go to the movies.* There are a growing number of films that also offer a peak into another world. They allow us to step outside our immediate circumstances to compare our experiences with

those in another context. Visit www.davidlivermore.com for some of my favorites.

- *Eat out.* Expand your horizons and try some different ethnic foods. If possible, share the meal with someone who comes from the culture of the food you're eating and see if he or she can offer some perspective about various dishes.

- *Journal.* Chronicle your cross-cultural observations, experiences, and questions. Don't write for an audience. Just write down your thoughts, feelings, and rants. Compare your expectations with your experiences and notice how your reflections change across time and situations.[21]

- *Learn a new language.* Take a language class or hire someone to tutor you. Then go somewhere and practice. Or check out a software program like Rosetta Stone or one of the language immersion programs offered many places around the world.

- *Attend cultural celebrations.* With the growing diversity occurring in most parts of the world, local ethnic celebrations are becoming more readily available to most of us. Locate an ethnic organization in a community near you and attend its cultural celebration. Say yes when invited to an ethnic wedding ceremony.

- *Go to the temple, mosque, or church.* Choose which one of these would be most *uncomfortable* for you to visit and go there. Be respectful, of course, and see if you can suspend your judgments about this religion's adherents. Just observe what's going on. Seek to understand this subculture.

- *Consume a variety of news sources.* Don't always get your news from the same place. If you have a favorite, fine, but branch out to see how other news sources report on the same event or story. And find sources that can keep you globally informed of the big events occurring around the world such as BBC news, public broadcasting, or www.worldpress.org.

- *Look for culture.* Continually keep your eyes open for how culture affects what you see. What might a company's website say about who they are? Why did a restaurant choose that logo?

Why do the homes in this neighborhood look like that?

- *Join a multicultural group.* Whether it's a reading group, musical band, or leadership roundtable, look for ways to socialize with ethnically diverse groups of people and observe how culture shapes the way each person engages.

- *Take an acting class.* Actors often invest weeks and even months in researching the life of a character they're going to portray on-stage. They have a great deal to teach us about how to adapt our behavior cross-culturally.

- *Find a cultural coach.* Find someone who understands the challenges of bridging the cultures where you have the greatest struggles. Or at the very least, find a peer who will join you in the journey toward enhanced CQ.

- *Take a class.* Formal courses and training on culture or on various regions of the world can play a significant role in enhancing our cultural experiences. The best courses include some kind of immersion in various cultural contexts where you actually spend time interacting with people from that culture.

- *Travel.* There are many fun, safe, and relatively inexpensive places where you can vacation or study without spending a ton of money. Scope out the local haunts, walk the streets, shop the local markets, and take in as much of the local culture as you can without being a nuisance.

- *Read the local paper when you travel.* Seek out a *local* English newspaper wherever you go. Skim all of it—advertisements, classifieds, public notices. You can gain fascinating insight into a place by reading what gets reported in the local news. Even check out the obituaries.

- *Create a faith club.* Engage in interfaith dialogue with people from other religions. Read books by people with whom you're likely to disagree.[22]

- *Create taboo lists.* Write down the words and behaviors to avoid in a particular culture with which you work. Keep this list some-where close by so you can add to it and review it as needed.

- *Go to the museum.* Visit a museum and learn about the history or art of various cultures. Attend a lecture about the history or literature of a place where you work.
- *Role-play.* Choose a behavior different from how you would typically do something (e.g., eating with your hands or speaking very close to someone) and practice doing it. Get a group of friends and try it together.
- *Talk to taxi drivers.* Ask taxi drivers for their perspective on local events. Some of my best insights into a place have come from them. They know the city and they encounter all kinds of people. Learn from them!
- *Take public transit.* Even if you only go a couple of stops, hop on the train or bus to travel the way a huge percentage of locals do. Try the Observe/Interpret exercise as you travel (refer back to Figure 6-1).
- *Stroll through the grocery store.* Even if you don't buy anything, stop at the local store. Notice what kinds of food are for sale, how it's displayed, and who's doing the shopping.
- *Question, question, question.* Ask questions. Listen hard. Ask questions. Listen hard. Ask questions. Listen hard. I can't think of anything more crucial toward the journey of cultural intelligence than this point. Continually ask questions of yourself. Continually ask questions of others. And listen for what's said in response (and what's *not* said!).
- *Identify your weakest dimension of CQ (drive, knowledge, strategy, or action).* Refer back to the best practices listed at the end of the corresponding chapter for the step that's hardest for you. Start there.

The possibilities keep going. These practices have limited value without the fuller explanation of how they fit with the cultural intelligence framework. But it's important to see cultural intelligence need not be an overwhelming, time-consuming pursuit. Many of these activities can fit in with our existing schedule and activities.

HOW TO BECOME MORE CULTURALLY INTELLIGENT

Step 1: CQ Drive

- Be honest with yourself.
- Examine your confidence level.
- Eat and socialize.
- Count the perks.
- Work for the triple bottom line.

Step 2: CQ Knowledge

- See culture's role in yourself and others.
- Review the basic cultural systems.
- Learn the core cultural values.
- Understand different languages.

Step 3: CQ Strategy

- Become more aware.
- Plan your cross-cultural interactions.
- Check to see if your assumptions and plans were appropriate.

Step 4: CQ Action

- Adapt your communication.
- Negotiate differently.
- Know when to flex and when not to flex.

Conclusion

Simon recently told me that he doesn't need any more ammunition to believe in the value of cultural intelligence. He's seen it in his own leadership and company. He's now into his second year of owning the company he acquired. He's leading a globally dispersed team of trainers and coaches across fifteen countries and the company just had its best year of financial gains. I'd be the first to acknowledge numerous factors that have contributed to Simon's success. But when surveying his personnel across fifteen countries, their evaluation of Simon's leadership was that he possesses an unusual ability to offer a compelling, unifying vision across the company while allowing each unit's members to contextualize their work as they see best. It's hard to believe this is the same leader I heard described as "inauthentic and manipulative" by his New England colleagues.

Cultural intelligence is directly tied to personal and organizational performance. A number of factors shape an individual's CQ, but everyone can grow in the journey toward becoming more effective cross-culturally. Dinner and a movie, a taxi ride, and a stroll through the grocery store are some simple ways to start developing your CQ this week.

CHAPTER 9

RECRUIT TRAVEL COMPANIONS: DEVELOPING
CQ IN YOUR TEAM

Cultural intelligence is an important skill set for anyone living and working in the twenty-first-century world, but it's essential for leaders in order to *lead*. Profitable and sustainable businesses need executives who understand diverse markets. Successful military missions depend on officers who can lead their personnel to engage strategically. Charitable causes need globally minded leaders who can work across national borders effectively.

If leaders don't become culturally intelligent, they'll be managed by the cultures where they work rather than leading by their guiding values and objectives.[1] Most of the book has focused on the personal development of cultural intelligence for those of us in leadership roles. But as we discover the personal benefits of cultural intelligence, we inevitably want to see it become a guiding influence all throughout our organizations. This final chapter covers a number of key strategies for leading a culturally intelligent organization.

Integrate CQ with Your Overall Mission

Leading an organization toward becoming more culturally intelligent starts with wedding cultural intelligence with your overall mission. Rather than make CQ an ancillary issue and consideration, weave the thread of respectful and effective global engagement right into the very fabric of your organizational vision. This might mean redefining what "success" means for your organization.

Include measurements for social responsibility and respect along-side financial targets. Don't underestimate the connection between the two. Permeate your strategic plan with action steps that move you toward more culturally intelligent behavior. Instead of being stretched and overrun by globalization and virtual work teams, tap into the strengths and opportunities that exist within these twenty-first-century realities.

Imagine being an organization that not only survives in the unpredictable, chaotic world of globalization but actually thrives in it. Develop a vision for defying the abysmal statistics that predict a 70 percent failure rate among all international ventures. And believe that culturally intelligent leaders and organizations enjoy tangible and altruistic profits that far outweigh the costs. As demonstrated in the research cited throughout this book, the economic value added by integrating cultural intelligence into your leadership role and into your organization is proven again and again. Join a movement of leaders who are making cultural intelligence the modus operandi for twenty-first-century leadership by making it central to your mission, vision, and values.

Build Commitment with Senior Leaders

Unless senior leaders embody the values and vision of your organization, those ideas remain mere words on a PowerPoint presentation or Web page. This is especially true when embracing a vision for becoming a more culturally intelligent force in the world. The level of CQ among senior leaders is the most consistent variable linked to whether or not an organization functions in the world with a track record of dignity, respect, and social responsibility. Senior leaders have to prioritize cultural intelligence in order to see it become a guiding characteristic and modus operandi throughout the organization as a whole. Coping and responding to fast-changing circumstances and the enactment of a global strategy rests on a team of senior leaders who can draw on the four-step cycle of cultural intelligence.[2]

Begin by painting a picture for your leaders of what it looks like to become a more culturally intelligent organization. Some of the questions I consistently use when talking with senior leaders about this include the following:

- What are your key performance goals?
- What are the biggest challenges hindering you from reaching those goals?
- In what way does culture play a part in your challenges (e.g., a dispersed workforce, multicultural teams, culturally diverse markets, expatriate assignments, short-term travel)?

Communicate the ways cultural intelligence can help address some of the key roadblocks facing your team. Explain the four-step cycle of the cultural intelligence model and regularly run through it with cultural situations facing you as a leader. Have each leader complete a CQ assessment (more information available at http://www.cq-portal.com).

Next, develop a collaborative plan for making cultural intelligence nonnegotiable in your organizational future. This can't simply be relegated to a department like human resources or international operations. The senior leaders have to personally forge the way in leading with cultural intelligence. CQ has to be woven throughout each part of the organization.

Fill the Organization with CQ Team Members

Although individuals in senior positions of leadership have to lead the way in embracing and prioritizing cultural intelligence, eventually most of the personnel throughout an organization need some measure of cultural intelligence. The greater the degree of cultural distance encountered by team members in their daily work, the more important it is for them to understand and grow in cultural intelligence. Therefore, the most obvious positions where cultural intelligence should become a required skill set among your team include international project managers, expatriate assignments, and representatives who are expected to travel internationally on your behalf.

Consider how to develop cultural intelligence even among employees who don't fill the kinds of positions that have direct responsibility for negotiating and working cross-culturally. The vision and values of your organization are ultimately whatever experience a customer has any time she encounters one of your team members. The support person answering e-mails and returning phone calls *is* your organization to the individual on the other end of that e-mail or phone call. The faculty member behind closed doors in the classroom *is* your university to his students. The nurse treating the immigrant *is* your hospital to that patient and her family. Reflecting cultural intelligence in the way you write your mission statement, market your products, or share your vision is important. However, it pales in contrast with the role your personnel play in communicating how your organization functions among people of difference. The way your team behaves cross-culturally reflects as much on your entire organization as it does on them personally. Begin by assessing the degree to which cultural intelligence is important for various functions in the organization. Two roles where CQ is extremely important are human resource personnel and those who have to travel and work internationally.

Human Resource Personnel

There are few departments for whom cultural intelligence has as much direct relevance to their day-to-day work as the human resource department. Don't hire a human resource director who doesn't have strong CQ! Human resource personnel are going to need CQ to analyze and fill various jobs within the organization and for hiring practices, performance appraisals, training, and career planning.[3] The four-step cycle offers human resource officers a consistent model for everything from promoting respect among a diverse workforce to creating policies that attend to religious and cultural diversity among personnel. Human resource directors need cultural intelligence to develop it in others and for screening, recruiting, and developing individuals for work assignments that include international travel. The human resource office is a strategic place to begin nurturing cultural intelligence.

International Travelers

Project managers who come into daily contact with suppliers and customers in international markets should be expected to have higher levels of CQ in all four dimensions than those who work primarily in the domestic market. Many of these individuals will have to travel into these markets. And CQ is most needed by staff deployed for extended overseas assignments. Don't just recruit individuals with the technical competence for the job; they should have stronger CQ than individuals who fill the same kind of position at home. Pay attention to team members and candidates who demonstrate unusual self-efficacy for cross-cultural assignments. Assess their CQ and give careful consideration to either screening out candidates who don't or finding ways to help them develop and grow. This can save you thousands and sometimes millions of dollars. Don't miss this one! Just because someone is a great engineer in Atlanta doesn't mean the person will perform well as an engineer in Dubai.

After carefully selecting an individual for an international assignment, offer the person ongoing training and development. Don't just do pre-departure training. Clearly, there's some information and awareness needed on the front end. The emphasis in pre-departure orientation should be on learning how to survive during the first six months and learning what questions to ask. But there's often a much higher level of motivation for learning about cultural intelligence midway through an international assignment rather than at the beginning. Too much pre-departure training can feel irrelevant and theoretical to individuals who are mostly trying to figure out how to pack up their homes and move to the other side of the world. But after being engaged in a foreign assignment for a while, a whole new set of questions emerges along with a pent-up desire to find solutions to working and living overseas. This is a far better time to offer more thorough training in cultural intelligence than inoculating employees with too much at the front end.

Screen Candidates for CQ

In order to fill positions with culturally intelligent personnel, assess them in the four dimensions of CQ. In addition to administering a CQ assessment, questions to explore when interviewing, observing, and checking references include the following:

CQ DRIVE
- ☐ To what degree does she show an interest in different cultures?
- ☐ Has she sought out opportunities to work with colleagues from different backgrounds?
- ☐ Does she appear confident she can succeed in cross-cultural situations?

CQ KNOWLEDGE
- ☐ Does he demonstrate insight into how culture influences his decision making?
- ☐ Can he describe the basic cultural differences that exist among the cultures where the organization works?
- ☐ Does he speak another language?

CQ STRATEGY

- ☐ How does she demonstrate awareness of herself and others?
- ☐ Does she plan differently for cross-cultural interactions and work?
- ☐ Does she check back to see if her cross-cultural behavior is effective?

CQ ACTION

- ☐ Can he alter his communication for various contexts?
- ☐ Does he demonstrate flexible negotiation skills?
- ☐ To what degree does he flex his behavior when working with people and projects in different cultural contexts?

Whether promoting someone to a new role or hiring someone externally, these are essential considerations. As mentioned previously, two of the key roles where a high level of CQ should be considered nonnegotiable are human resource personnel and individuals who will need to travel internationally.

Reward Good CQ Performance

Finally, celebrate the diversity that exists within your own workforce and provide incentives for culturally intelligent behavior. Keep in mind the cultural and individual differences in what motivates various team members. For some, financial remuneration is the most compelling incentive while for others it might be job fulfillment, job security, flextime, or status. Challenge your team to embrace a transcendent motivation for treating people with dignity and respect and for making the world a better place. Give them a vision for being a community of individuals who are committed to the greater good and to being an agent for respectful and humane global engagement. Here's something you might consider: Growing numbers of organizations are giving employees one week of paid time to do volunteer tourism somewhere in the world.

They realize the payoff that comes from having employees travel to another part of the world and the ways it allows the organization to contribute to something bigger than itself. In return, employees tap into one of the greatest tools for becoming more culturally intelligent — international travel.[4] One Los Angeles–based manufacturing company has created a foundation wherein the company helps provide clean water filters for several communities throughout Sub-Saharan Africa. They also offer employees one week of paid time to do volunteer service in one of these regions. And employees can even apply for grant money from the company's foundation to help fund their trips. The CEO and employees both find great return on this investment.

Determine the areas where it's most important to have culturally intelligent personnel and work with your human resource department to ensure those positions are filled with culturally intelligent individuals. The cost of senior leadership's time and lost opportunities from not doing so is too expensive. Join the organizations on the front edge of leading in a diverse world that see cultural intelligence as a driving priority for personnel.

Develop CQ Strategies

Although having culturally intelligent personnel is essential for gaining the benefits of cultural intelligence, it's not the end all. Your organization also needs to develop CQ strategies. These are the tactical procedures and routines that exist throughout the organization to enable it to function day-to-day in culturally intelligent ways. As you identify your desired milestones and map out specific plans for getting there, be sure to ask how global and cultural realities will affect these plans. I'm amazed at the number of organizations I encounter that launch full initiatives without any careful assessment of how this initiative will play out differently in various cultural markets. When a vendor pitches you a service based on vast market research, ask for the demographics of the research sample. Or if you're reading a report about the characteristics, needs, and interests of adolescents, be sure to ask, what adolescents? Are they adolescents everywhere? American adolescents? What American adolescents—white, middle-class, suburban youth or urban Hispanic, inner-city youth? This kind of careful reflection about the role of culture in how you form your strategic plan will shape how you allocate resources (money, personnel, land, facilities, and equipment) to achieve your goals.

One U.S.-based office furniture company reported huge interest from Japan in its new line of desks and chairs. The company immediately shipped two containers full of the furniture to Japan, rented prime space in downtown Tokyo for a display room, and then watched the furniture sit on display with very limited sales. Lots of people would come in and try sitting at the desks but few sold. Much later, they discovered that the chairs, which were designed for larger Americans, were uncomfortable to the smaller-framed Japanese. And the large desks symbolized a pretense unwanted by Japanese executives. The company shipped all the furniture back home and worked with some Japanese engineers to redesign its product specifically with Asian customers in mind. Five years later, it was the largest office furniture distributor in Asia.

The ways we view R&D, strategic planning, production, marketing, and assessment are all deeply rooted in our cultural systems and values. The process we use to arrive at decisions, the assumptions we make for how production will happen, and the marketing plans we see as innovative and effective are all a reflection of culture. So as we develop a culturally intelligent team around us, we have to think strategically about what a good marketing plan looks like in Mexico so we don't end up with a whole campaign that reads, "Are you lactating?" instead of "Got milk?"

If you develop a production timeline that assumes you can reach a contract with a subsidiary in China in time to meet a deadline, you'd best tap into cultural intelligence to determine how to negotiate in a way that will appeal to the values of Chinese businesses. And when selecting a cross-border partner, you need to identify the key competitive factors associated with working together, assess the cultural and organizational risks connected with each of these factors, and draw on these in your corporate decision making.[5] Culturally intelligent strategies help us identify, plan for, and manage risks beforehand as well as on the fly when the unexpected happens—and it will!

Form CQ Structures

Next, we need to create appropriate structures and mechanisms for enacting CQ strategies. CQ knowledge helps us form structures that consider the role of varying cultural systems (e.g., legal and religious) and values (e.g., time and power distance) for how we work in different markets. For example, although the system used for negotiating contracts needs some uniformity throughout your organization, it also needs to be flexible enough to realistically reach a contract in various cultures. You have to figure out how to retain legal and fiscal responsibility (e.g., a signed contract) while also accommodating the informal, unofficial approaches to negotiation used in many less industrial countries. The differences in the maturity of legal frameworks for contract law, property rights, and arbitration procedures are precisely why culturally intelligent structures are necessary.[6] Refer back to the leadership implications of the cultural systems and values described in Chapters 4 and 5.

Another reason to develop CQ structures is to accommodate the geographical distance that exists between offices and affiliates across an organization. This distance often results in time zone differences and disparity in telecommunication infrastructures, the scope of knowledge sources, and the scale of a partner's business. A culturally intelligent structure across physical distance might include a roaming schedule for conference calls among regional leaders so everyone can share the inconvenient time slots. A simple adaptation like this one goes a long way to building a culturally intelligent organization.

Universities that draw large populations of international students provide another way to think about the need for culturally intelligent structures. International students usually come with a different set of academic and personal needs than home culture students have. Culturally intelligent structures are needed to help them succeed. Similar kinds of flexible structures are needed for the varying religious beliefs and practices held by diverse faculty and students.

One of the challenges for the culturally intelligent organization is to develop malleable structures while not reinventing the entire process every time you move into a new cultural context. Customizing and adapting structures is essential, but it's unsustainable to build a new structure for each situation. And at some point, completely re-creating your structures and product line for every context can result in losing your brand identity altogether. McDonald's fries and shakes taste pretty similar in Chicago and Delhi. There's some uniformity to the experience of eating at McDonald's most anywhere. But the localized approaches to menus demonstrate some flexible structures within McDonald's international approach. The flavor of shakes available in Chicago and Delhi restaurants is different. And the basic McDonald's product—the hamburger—isn't available at its Indian stores. McDonald's has developed a structure that can demonstrate respect for the Hindu convictions toward eating beef. So instead of the Big Mac, the McVeggie is at the center of the McDonald's menu in India. As flexible structures, services, and products are developed and morphed, your team is allowed to function in culturally intelligent and productive ways.

Create CQ Decision-Making Systems

The process of decision making is another key element of becoming a more culturally intelligent organization. Each organization has its own process of decision making, which works in tandem with the national cultures of which the organization is a part. Some organizational cultures use a decision-making model that places primary interest in establishing norms and shaping the industry or market. For example, Apple Computer's foray into producing portable music players and cell phones demonstrated an organizational culture intent on redefining how people listen to music and use a mobile phone. These kinds of cultures don't base their decisions primarily on what the market currently says it likes. Instead, these organizations want to create a new norm in the cultures where they work. On the other hand, many other organizational cultures are characterized by being primarily market driven and pragmatic. These businesses look at what's currently a successful trend and offer a product that taps into that market.

Another difference in decision-making approaches are organizations that base their decisions on data and research versus those that make decisions more intuitively or based on an edict from a senior leader in the organization. Still other organizational cultures wed research with a more intuitive sense of chemistry about something while others are highly democratic and incentivize employees and constituents to offer innovative ideas. It's certainly appropriate for an organization to develop and retain its own organizational decision-making style, but this approach may need to be adapted when moving in and out of different ethnic cultures.

Culturally intelligent teams ask, how do we learn which innovations are worthy of our investment and energy when considering culturally different markets? And how do the various cultures and regions of our team influence how we decide? Develop an overall decision-making process that helps your team balance an appropriate measure of self-governing authority while also knowing where to get help when confounded by the unanticipated curve-balls that come with multicultural leadership.

Facilitate a CQ Learning Plan

Although training shouldn't be the only method used to implement CQ, it is an important facet. Effectively learning about cultural intelligence begins with CQ drive. Mandating that employees sit through training on diversity or cross-border negotiation doesn't ensure an interested audience. For those of us who step into learning situations where people are required to participate, we have to make a more convincing case for why individuals should care about cultural intelligence. Connections need to be made between cultural intelligence and their personal interests. In the following section, I offer a few suggestions for educating your team about cultural intelligence.

Show-and-Tell

Gather your team members and explain the benefits of CQ to them personally and to the organization as a whole. Conversely, communicate the corresponding costs for cultural ignorance. Use the findings reported in this book to demonstrate the payoffs of CQ. Talk about the connection between cultural intelligence and their goals rather than just talking about cultural intelligence as an end in itself. In so doing, you're tapping into the CQ drive element before immediately jumping into the cognitive issues of cultural intelligence. Teach the four-step cycle as a model to use in any cross-cultural situation.

Give them a copy of this book and have them complete a CQ assessment. Begin to interest them in getting more understanding about how cultural intelligence can help them enhance their career and prevent them from vocational obsolescence.

Divisional Training

With the exception of something like the show-and-tell approach, I don't recommend doing much one-size-fits-all training on cultural intelligence. As your senior leadership joins you in embracing the value and priority of cultural intelligence, find ways to incorporate learning about cultural intelligence throughout your leaders' respective areas in the organization. The sales team has a whole different framework from which to approach cultural intelligence than the R&D team does. The same is true for marketing. There are clearly some times when cross-functional training is valuable to avoid perpetuating the silo effect. But I find most employees grow frustrated if cultural intelligence is simply taught in an overarching, ambiguous way rather than customizing its application to specific roles and functions in the organization. Senior leaders can usually handle broader discussions about cultural intelligence at the 30,000-foot view. But those functioning in various units typically prefer to have concepts like cultural intelligence directly applied to their work in concrete terms. Put primary energy into offering divisional expertise on the application of cultural intelligence to the various functions of your teams.

Personal CQ Development Plan

Several organizations ask their employees at all levels to complete a personal development plan at their annual performance review. Include cultural intelligence as an area where personnel need to identify a growth plan for the next year. Offer coaching on ways they can make some progress in cultural intelligence during the next year. The more the plan aligns with their personal motivation and interests, the better. Ask them for one objective for each of the four steps—measurable tasks to grow their motivation, knowledge, strategy, and actions.

At one large company, employees complete a Measurable

Annual Performance Plan each year. Individuals can choose from a variety of course offerings as part of fulfilling their objectives. Several employees take a two-day class on global business that's offered as a way of doing this. The course introduces participants to new perspectives and techniques that bridge organizational, national, and cultural boundaries to meet customer demands worldwide. Participants learn how to achieve more effective cross-cultural business relationships and ultimately to improve global performance.[7]

You might also consider making course offerings on country-specific knowledge available, particularly if your organization works mostly in a small number of other regions. Or offer skill-based courses on how to negotiate cross-culturally and walk the negotiation process through the four steps. Think about offering a series of trainings on various communication behaviors needed like those examined in Chapter 7. For example, you could help your team practice how to give and receive compliments in various places, how to make requests, express apologies, and learn appropriate topics of conversation. Some companies have even brought in spiritual directors to teach personnel how to develop the skill of awareness, a key part of gaining CQ strategy. The best practices listed at the ends of Chapters 3 to 7 will give you many more ideas of things to use with your team. Language learning, book clubs, international travel, and vocal coaching can all be strategies you offer your team for growing in cultural intelligence. There are many resources available to help individuals learn new ways of seeing and doing things in a variety of contexts.[8]

The most important way to nurture and develop cultural intelligence throughout the organization is by personally modeling it. The goal is not to feel some pressure to become a master teacher in cultural intelligence who never gets frustrated or makes mistakes. Instead, demonstrate a high value for the strategic benefits of cultural intelligence to you as a leader, to the organization, and to the greater good of humanity. Describe the relevance of the four-step cycle of cultural intelligence to something you're doing. And model the value of learning from mistakes. In fact, the use of negative experiences as a source of inspiration for change is evidence of high CQ. When encountering a new culture, you will inevitably experience some failure and setbacks. The critical issue is not flawless behavior but how we learn from our mistakes and negative experiences. High CQ helps us pay attention to what we can learn from both good and bad experiences cross-culturally.[9]

Nurture a community of lifelong learners for working and living in our multicultural world. Find creative ways to inspire and educate your team to grow in cultural intelligence. Provide lots of encouragement and empower your team members to take ownership of some of your emerging initiatives in new cultural markets.[10] Guide them through it and help them apply cultural intelligence to the assignment. As you do so, you're giving them a skill set that allows them to tap into the unprecedented opportunities of the twenty-first-century world. And your organization will have a decided edge for staying ahead of the curve in our fast-paced world.

Conclusion

With every quarter that goes by, the importance of leading with cultural intelligence becomes more and more significant. You can have all the right policies and make all the right tactical decisions, but if you don't engage with cultural intelligence, forget it! Accomplishing your performance objectives will be a crapshoot at best and you have a 70 percent chance of failure.

Just look at one of the most powerful leaders at the beginning of this century—President George W. Bush. No president in U.S. history has been more pro-Indian than George Bush. He negotiated policies that offered marketable opportunities for India that far outweighed what his predecessor, President Bill Clinton, ever did. Bill Clinton issued far more sanctions against India and condemned India for the country's underground nuclear weapons. Yet on the whole, Clinton is loved by India far more than Bush. Clinton's trips to India always involved getting up close with the people and the culture. The Bush administration, on the other hand, kept the president from any substantive interaction with Indian people besides government officials. As was typical in most of his foreign trips, he had limited engagement with business leaders, civil servants, and activists when he visited India as president. Admittedly, the security issues of a post-9/11 era put him at much greater risk than previous U.S. presidents experienced. But fair or not, the limited interaction between Bush and the people and the culture of the places he traveled communicated a lack of respect and appreciation. That may not have been his intent, but sometimes it's *not* just the thought that counts. If he had been able to make a broader effort to touch the people in the foreign lands he visited, there would have been significant symbolic value. This is an extreme example of how the policy decisions of a leader matter, but the symbolism surrounding a leader's cross-cultural interactions are often far more powerful.[11] Many organizational leaders do the same thing. They make some great strides in developing good international plans and partnerships, but by failing to truly engage with the people and culture connected to those plans, the partnership brings far fewer results than it could.

By tapping into the emerging domain of cultural intelligence, you and your organization need not be one more statistic of failure in international work. Cultural intelligence offers us a realistic approach to the frenetic travel schedules and deadlines we face as leaders. It's an ongoing skill set that grows as we continue to live, lead, and learn. And it provides a way to stay ahead of the curve while also contributing to the greater good of humanity in the world.

Follow the four-step cycle toward CQ as you prepare for your next cross-cultural interaction:

- Step 1: Examine your motivation (CQ drive).
- Step 2: Seek to understand (CQ knowledge).
- Step 3: Think outside the box as you plan (CQ strategy).
- Step 4: Effectively lead with respect (CQ action).

I'm about to make my first trip to Sudan. My wanderlust serves my CQ drive well. I'm intrigued to walk the streets of a place I've heard so much about. I rarely feel nervous about anywhere I travel but there is some measure of reticence given all the violence that continues there. But I can see some networking opportunities this trip is going to give me and that helps to motivate me. I'm stopping in Dubai en route to explore a new partnership there and that further increases my interest in taking this upcoming trip. I've followed the recent history of Sudan through the news and through books like Dave Egger's *What Is the What*. I've had Sudanese students in class. But I have very little depth of knowledge on the ins and outs of Sudanese culture. But I'm not starting from scratch. My CQ knowledge about cultures in general gives me a set of questions I'm thinking through as I anticipate doing my work there. And I'm drawing on a growing portfolio of understanding to plan and strategize how I'm going to go about my consulting and teaching role while I'm there. CQ strategy is helping me be mindful of how I'll be perceived. I'm thinking about the degree to which I can fairly apply what I've experienced in other East African cultures to Sudan.

At the end of the day, I expect my behavior in Sudan (CQ action) will be a mixed bag of successes and failures. It usually is. I want to prepare well. But I don't want to overthink it. I can't really. There's way too much I have to do between now and when I leave for Sudan. So how can I be a responsible leader in keeping ahead of the curve through the twists and turns of the multidimensional world in Sudan while not getting stuck in the paralysis of analysis? Cultural intelligence offers me a manageable way forward. I'm not just winging it but neither am I setting myself up for the unrealistic sense that I can spend the next few weeks becoming an expert on Sudanese culture. So much for Sudan—I have a conference call in ten minutes with affiliates from the Czech Republic, Mexico, the United States, and China. It's time to leave the flat, predictable terrain of book writing and get back to leading and relating in the multidimensional world awaiting me. See you along the way!

APPENDIX: RESEARCH CONTEXT

The cultural intelligence model is rooted in rigorous empirical work that spans researchers from twenty-five countries. Christopher Earley and Soon Ang built on the research on multiple intelligences to develop the conceptual model of cultural intelligence.[1] Researchers Soon Ang, Linn Van Dyne, Christine Koh, Koh-Yee Ng, Klaus Templer, Cheryl Tay, and N. Anand Chandrasekar developed and validated a twenty-item inventory, called the Cultural Intelligence Scale (CQS), to measure CQ across multiple cultures.[2] Since 2003, the topic of CQ has attracted significant attention worldwide and across diverse disciplines. According to Soon Ang and Linn Van Dyne, the research has been presented to many groups, including the Society for Industrial and Organizational Psychology, American Psychological Association, International Conference on Information Systems, International Academy of Intercultural Relations, International Congress of Applied Psychology, Shanghai Conference on Cultural Intelligence in China, United States Defense Advanced Research Projects Agency, and International Military Testing Association.[3] Although most thoroughly tested in business and educational contexts, data have also been collected from the fields of nursing, engineering, law, consulting, mental health, government, and religion.

The research referenced throughout the book comes from a number of the researchers engaged in testing cultural intelligence, including myself. Any of the data drawn directly from the research of others are cited as such. The remaining cultural intelligence findings included in the book come from data I collected from 2005 to 2008, as part of the Cultural Intelligence and Leadership Project. This project was a series of studies that tested and applied cultural intelligence to the work of leaders across a variety of professional contexts: business, educational, charitable, and government. The hypothesis of the Cultural Intelligence and Leadership Project is that a positive relationship exists between the acquisition of cultural intelligence and leaders' effectiveness in the twenty-first century. To date, 1,023 subjects have been involved in this research project. Data were collected using a grounded-theory approach through interviewing subjects, reading subject journals, administering surveys, convening focus groups, and making firsthand observations. These studies were intended to be descriptive in nature.

A subset of this research included testing religious leaders' experiences with not only socioethnic culture but also organizational and generational culture, the findings of which are found in my book *Cultural Intelligence: Improving Your CQ to Engage Our Multicultural World*. Most of the data for this subset were collected through focus-group research.

To respect and protect the confidentiality of the subjects surveyed, their names and the names of their organizations have been changed; however, other demographic information (e.g., gender, age, ethnicity, and basic location) have not been altered in the reporting of the findings here and elsewhere. I'm extremely grateful for the generosity of hundreds of leaders and their organizations for entrusting me with some of their thoughts, sentiments, and reflections about cross-cultural leadership. Visit the Cultural Intelligence Center at http://www.cq-portal.com for more information on CQ research.

Preface

1. Soon Ang and Linn Van Dyne, "Conceptualization of Cultural Intelligence" in *Handbook of Cultural Intelligence: Theory, Measurement, and Applications,* Soon Ang and Linn Van Dyne, eds. (Armonk, NY: M.E. Sharpe, 2008), 3.
2. Aimin Yan and Yadong Luo, *International Joint Ventures: Theory and Practice* (Armonk, NY: M.E. Sharpe, 2000), 32.
3. R. Sternberg and Douglas K. Detterman, *What Is Intelligence? Contemporary Viewpoints on Its Nature and Definition* (New York: Ablex Publishing, 1986).
4. Soon Ang, Linn Van Dyne, Christine Koh, Koh-Yee Ng, Klaus Templer, Swing Ling Cheryl Tay, and N. Anand Chandrasekar, "Cultural Intelligence: Its Measurement and Effects on Cultural Judgment and Decision-Making, Cultural Adaptation, and Task Performance," *Management and Organization Review* 3 (2007): 335–371.
5. A compilation of much of the CQ research conducted to date is reported in Soon Ang and Linn Van Dyne, eds., *Handbook of Cultural Intelligence: Theory, Measurement, and Applications* (Armonk, NY: M.E. Sharpe, 2008).

Chapter 1   You Lead Across a Multicultural Terrain: Why CQ?

1. Soon Ang and Linn Van Dyne, "Conceptualization of Cultural Intelligence" in *Handbook of Cultural Intelligence: Theory, Measurement, and Applications,* Soon Ang and Linn Van Dyne, eds. (Armonk, NY: M.E. Sharpe, 2008), 3.
2. Thomas Friedman, *The World Is Flat: A Brief History of the Twenty-First Century* (New York: Farrar, Straus & Giroux, 2005).
3. Economist Intelligence Unit, "CEO Briefing: Corporate Priorities for 2006 and Beyond" in *The Economist: Economic Intelligence Unit*

(EIU) at http://a330.g.akamai.net/7/330/25828/20060213195601/ graphics.eiu.com/files/ad_pdfs/ceo_Briefing_UKTI_wp.pdf, 3.

4. Ibid., 5.
5. Ibid., 9.
6. Gary Ferraro, *The Cultural Dimension of Business* (Upper Saddle River, NJ: Prentice-Hall, 1990), 2–3.
7. Economist Intelligence Unit, "CEO Briefing," 9.
8. Ibid., 17.
9. Douglas A. Ready, Linder A. Hill, and Jay A. Conger, "Winning the Race for Talent in Emerging Markets," *Harvard Business Review* (November 2008): 63–70.
10. Jessica R. Mesmer-Magnus and Chockalingham Viswesvaran, "Expatriate Management: A Review and Directions for Research in Expatriate Selection, Training, and Repatriation" in *Handbook of Research in International Human Resource Management,* Michael Harris, ed. (Boca Raton, FL: CRC Press, 2007), 184; and Linda J. Stroh, J. Stewart Black, Mark E. Mendenhall, and Hal B. Gregersen, *International Assignments: An Integration of Strategy, Research, and Practice* (Boca Raton, FL: CRC Press, 2004).
11. Margaret Shaffer and Gloria Miller, "Cultural Intelligence: A Key Success Factor for Expatriates" in *Handbook of Cultural Intelligence: Theory, Measurement, and Applications,* Soon Ang and Linn Van Dyne, eds. (Armonk, NY: M.E. Sharpe, 2008), 107, 120.
12. R. J. House, P. J. Hanges, M. Javidan, P. W. Dorfman, and V. Gupta, *Culture, Leadership and Organizations: The GLOBE Study of 62 Societies* (Thousand Oaks, CA: Sage, 2004), 12.
13. Kok Yee Ng, Linn Van Dyne, and Soon Ang, "From Experience to Experiential Learning: Cultural Intelligence as a Learning Capability for Global Leader Development," *Academy of Management Learning & Education* (forthcoming).
14. Soon Ang, Linn Van Dyne, C. Koh, K. Y. Ng, K. J. Templer, C. Tay, and N. A. Chandrasekar, "Cultural Intelligence: Its Measurement and Effects on Cultural Judgment and Decision-Making, Cultural Adaptation, and Task Performance," *Management and Organization Review* 3 (2007): 340.
15. Ibid.

Chapter 2   You Need a Map for the Journey: CQ Overview

1. Cheryl Tay, Mina Westman, and Audrey Chia, "Antecedents and Consequences of Cultural Intelligence Among Short-Term Business Travelers" in *Handbook of Cultural Intelligence: Theory, Measurement, and Applications*, Soon Ang and Linn Van Dyne, eds. (Armonk, NY: M.E. Sharpe, 2008), 130.

2. Soon Ang and Linn Van Dyne, "Conceptualization of Cultural Intelligence" in *Handbook of Cultural Intelligence: Theory, Measurement, and Applications*, Soon Ang and Linn Van Dyne, eds. (Armonk, NY: M.E. Sharpe, 2008), 3.

3. Linn Van Dyne and Soon Ang, "The Sub-Dimensions of the Four-Factor Model of Cultural Intelligence," technical report for the Cultural Intelligence Center, 2008.

4. Ibid.

5. Ibid.

6. Ibid.

7. Ibid.

8. Ibid.

9. Soon Ang, Linn Van Dyne, C. Koh, K. Y. Ng, K. J. Templer, C. Tay, and N. A. Chandrasekar, "Cultural Intelligence: Its Measurement and Effects on Cultural Judgment and Decision-Making, Cultural Adaptation, and Task Performance," *Management and Organization Review* 3 (2007): 335–371.

10. Linn Van Dyne, Soon Ang, and Christine Koh, "Development and Validation of the CQS: The Cultural Intelligence Scale" in *Handbook of Cultural Intelligence: Theory, Measurement, and Applications*, Soon Ang and Linn Van Dyne, eds. (Armonk, NY: M.E. Sharpe, 2008), 16–38; see Appendices A to C, Cultural Intelligence Scale (CQS), 389–391.

11. Linn Van Dyne and Soon Ang, "The Sub-Dimensions of the Four-Factor Model of Cultural Intelligence."

12. J. D. Mayer and P. Salovey, "What Is Emotional Intelligence?" in *Emotional Development and Emotional Intelligence: Educational Applications*, P. Salovey and D. Sluter, eds. (New York: Basic Books, 1997), 3–31.

13. Kok Yee Ng, Linn Van Dyne, and Soon Ang, "From Experience to Experiential Learning: Cultural Intelligence as a Learning

Capability for Global Leader Development," *Academy of Management Learning & Education* (forthcoming).

14. Soon Ang, Linn Van Dyne, and Christine Koh, "Personality Correlates of the Four-Factor Model of Cultural Intelligence," *Group & Organizational Management* 31 (2006): 100–123.

15. Maddy Janssens and Tineke Cappellen, "Contextualizing Cultural Intelligence: The Case of Global Managers" in *Handbook of Cultural Intelligence: Theory, Measurement, and Applications*, Soon Ang and Linn Van Dyne, eds. (Armonk, NY: M.E. Sharpe, 2008), 369.

16. David Livermore, *Cultural Intelligence and Leadership Project* (Grand Rapids, MI: Global Learning Center, 2008), 12.

17. Linda Fenty, personal conversation, May 1, 2008.

Chapter 3 Whet Your Appetite: CQ Drive (Step 1)

1. Linn Van Dyne and Soon Ang, "The Sub-Dimensions of the Four-Factor Model of Cultural Intelligence," technical report for the Cultural Intelligence Center, 2008.

2. Albert Bandura, *Self-Efficacy: The Exercise of Control* (New York: W.H. Freeman, 1997), 15.

3. Klaus Templer, C. Tay, and N. A. Chandrasekar, "Motivational Cultural Intelligence, Realistic Job Preview, Realistic Living Conditions Preview, and Cross-Cultural Adjustment," *Group & Organization Management* 31 (February 1, 2006): 167–168.

4. P. Christopher Earley, Soon Ang, and Joo-Seng Tan, *CQ: Developing Cultural Intelligence at Work* (Stanford, CA: Stanford Business Books, 2006), 69.

5. Cheryl Tay, Mina Westman, and Audrey Chia, "Antecedents and Consequences of Cultural Intelligence Among Short-Term Business Travelers" in *Handbook of Cultural Intelligence: Theory, Measurement, and Applications*, Soon Ang and Linn Van Dyne, eds. (Armonk, NY: M.E. Sharpe, 2008), 130.

6. P. Christopher Earley, Soon Ang, and Joo-Seng Tan, *CQ*, 67–68.

7. Craig Storti, *The Art of Crossing Cultures* (Yarmouth, ME: Intercultural Press, 1990), 44.

8. J. Stewart Black and Hal B. Gregersen, "The Right Way to Manage Expats," *Harvard Business Review* 77 (March/April): 53.

9. David Livermore, *Cultural Intelligence and Leadership Project*

(Grand Rapids, MI: Global Learning Center, 2008), 22.

10. Evan West, "America's Greenest City," *Fast Company* (October 2008): 80.

11. Thich Nhat Hanh, *The Art of Power* (New York: Harper One, 2007), 68.

12. Paulo Freire, *Pedagogy of the Oppressed* (New York: Continuum, 1997), 97.

13. Fareed Zakaria, *The Post-American World* (New York: Norton Publishing, 2008), 224.

14. Ibid., 226.

15. Ibid., 257–258.

16. Henry Cloud, *Integrity: The Courage to Meet the Demands of Reality* (New York: Collins, 2006), 242.

17. Lu M. Shannon and Thomas M. Begley, "Antecedents of the Four-Factor Model of Cultural Intelligence" in *Handbook of Cultural Intelligence: Theory, Measurement, and Applications*, Soon Ang and Linn Van Dyne, eds. (Armonk, NY: M.E. Sharpe, 2008), 41–54; and Ibraiz Tarique and Riki Takeuchi, "Developing Cultural Intelligence: The Role of International Nonwork Experiences" in *Handbook of Cultural Intelligence: Theory, Measurement, and Applications*, Soon Ang and Linn Van Dyne, eds. (Armonk, NY: M.E. Sharpe, 2008), 56.

Chapter 4 Study the Topography: CQ Knowledge (Step 2a)

1. Allan Hall, Tom Bawden, and Sarah Butler, "Wal-Mart Pulls Out of Germany at a Cost of $1BLN," *The Times* (July 29, 2006).

2. Edgar Schein, *Organizational Culture and Leadership* (San Francisco: Jossey-Bass, 2004), 11.

3. Linn Van Dyne and Soon Ang, "The Sub-Dimensions of the Four-Factor Model of Cultural Intelligence," technical report for the Cultural Intelligence Center, 2008.

4. Claudia Strauss and Naomi Quinn, *A Cognitive Theory of Cultural Meaning* (Cambridge: Cambridge University Press, 1997), 253.

5. William Rugh, "If Saddam Had Been a Fulbrighter," *Christian Science Monitor* (November 2, 1995).

6. William Kiehl, *America's Dialogue with the World* (Washington, DC: Public Diplomacy Council, 2006), 42.

7. *Baywatch* at http://en.wikipedia.org/wiki/Baywatch (accessed August, 24, 2007).

8. Robert Parkin, *Kinship: An Introduction to Basic Concepts* (Malden, MA: Blackwell), 49.

9. Kwok Leung and Soon Ang, "Culture, Organizations, and Institutions" in *Cambridge Handbook of Culture, Organizations, and Work*, R. S. Bhagat and R. M. Steers, eds. (Cambridge, MA: Cambridge University Press, 2008), 26.

10. Max Weber, *The Protestant Ethic and the Spirit of Capitalism* (New York: Charles Scribner's Sons, 1958).

11. Kwok Leung and Soon Ang, "Culture, Organizations, and Institutions," 29.

12. Aihwa Ong, *Spirits of Resistance and Capitalist Discipline: Factory Women in Malaysia* (Albany: State University of New York Press, 1987), 101.

13. Paul Hiebert, *Anthropological Reflections on Missiological Issues* (Grand Rapids, MI: Baker Academic, 1994), 114.

14. Ibid., 113.

Chapter 5   Dig Beneath the Terrain: CQ Knowledge (Step 2b)

1. See Robert Levine, *How Every Culture Keeps Time Just a Little Bit Differently* (New York: Basic, 1997), 157; adapted from Edward Hall and M. R. Hall, *Understanding Cultural Differences: Germans, French, and Americans* (Yarmouth, ME: Intercultural Press, 1990), 190; Geert Hofstede, "Individualism, Power Distance, and Uncertainty Avoidance" in *Cultures and Organizations: Software of the Mind* (New York: McGraw-Hill, 1997), 5; visit http://www.geerthofstede .com for more information. (Hofstede assigned Singapore a very low score in uncertainty avoidance [9 points], but this is widely dis- puted. The dominant culture in risk is far more risk-averse than this score suggests.); also see R. J. House, P. J. Hanges, M. Javidan, P. W. Dorfman, and V. Gupta, *Culture, Leadership, and Organizations: The GLOBE Study of 62 Societies* (Thousand Oaks, CA: Sage, 2004) for more on cultural values and leadership.

2. My experience closely mirrors a simulation referenced in Craig Storti, *Cross-Cultural Dialogues* (Yarmouth, ME: Intercultural Press, 1994), 64. Storti's analysis helped my own thinking about the role of hierarchy in this encounter.

3. L. Robert Kohls and John Knight, *Developing Intercultural*

Awareness: A Cross-Cultural Training Handbook (Yarmouth, ME: Intercultural Press, 1994), 45.

4. Soon Ang, personal conversation (October 26, 2005); and M. J. Gelfand, L. Nishii, and J. Raver, "On the Nature and Importance of Cultural Tightness-Looseness," *Journal of Applied Psychology* 91 (2006): 1225–1244.

5. Gary Ferraro, *The Cultural Dimension of Business* (Upper Saddle River, NJ: Prentice-Hall, 1990), 12.

6. S. T. Shen, M. Wooley, and S. Prior, "Towards Culture-Centered Design," *Interacting with Computers* 18 (2006): 820–852.

7. Gary Ferraro, *The Cultural Dimension of Business*, 48.

8. Ibid., 49.

Chapter 6   Turn Off the Cruise Control: CQ Strategy (Step 3)

1. Linn Van Dyne and Soon Ang, "The Sub-Dimensions of the Four-Factor Model of Cultural Intelligence," technical report for the Cultural Intelligence Center, 2008.

2. Thich Nhat Hanh, *The Miracle of Mindfulness* (Boston: Beacon, 1999), 42–44.

3. Tom Rath, *StrengthsFinder 2.0: A New and Upgraded Edition of the Online Test from Gallup's Now, Discover Your Strengths* (Washington, DC: Gallup Press, 2007).

4. P. Christopher Earley, Soon Ang, and Joo-Seng Tan, *CQ: Developing Cultural Intelligence at Work* (Stanford, CA: Stanford University Press, 2006), 11.

5. P. Christopher Earley and Soon Ang, *Cultural Intelligence: Individual Interactions Across Cultures* (Stanford, CA: Stanford Business Books, 2003), 115.

6. Soon Ang and Linn Van Dyne, "Conceptualization of Cultural Intelligence" in *Handbook of Cultural Intelligence: Theory, Measurement, and Applications*, Soon Ang and Linn Van Dyne, eds. (Armonk, NY: M.E. Sharpe, 2008), 5.

7. Richard Brislin, R. Worthley, and Brent Macnab, "Cultural Intelligence: Understanding Behaviors That Serve People's Goals," *Group and Organization Management* 31 (February 1, 2006), 49.

8. Six Sigma Financial Services, "Determine the Root Cause: 5 Whys," http://finance.isixsigma.com/library/content/c020610a.asp.

9. Kok Yee Ng, Linn Van Dyne, and Soon Ang, "From Experience to Experiential Learning: Cultural Intelligence as a Learning

Capability for Global Leader Development," *Academy of Management Learning & Education* (forthcoming issue).

Chapter 7   Run, Walk, or Jog: CQ Action (Step 4)

1. Edward Stewart and Milton Bennett, *American Cultural Patterns: A Cross-Cultural Perspective* (Boston: Intercultural Press, 1991), 15.
2. Linn Van Dyne and Soon Ang, "The Sub-Dimensions of the Four-Factor Model of Cultural Intelligence," technical report for the Cultural Intelligence Center, 2008.
3. University of Phoenix is a for-profit institution that specializes in adult education with more than 345,000 students on 200 campuses.
4. Linn Van Dyne and Soon Ang, "The Sub-Dimensions of the Four-Factor Model of Cultural Intelligence."
5. Helen Spencer-Oatey, *Culturally Speaking* (London: Continuum Press, 2000), 236–237.
6. Adapted from Helen Spencer-Oatey's example of asking someone to wash the dishes in Helen Spencer-Oatey, *Culturally Speaking* (London: Continuum Press, 2000), 22.
7. Originally reported in my book *Cultural Intelligence: Improving Your CQ to Engage Our Multicultural World* (Grand Rapids, ME: Baker Books, 2008), 115.
8. Peter Hays Gries and Kaiping Peng, "Culture Clash? Apologies East and West," *Journal of Contemporary China* 11 (2002): 173–178.
9. David Thomas and Kerr Inkson, *Cultural Intelligence: People Skills for Global Business* (San Francisco: Berrett-Koehler, 2004), 113.
10. Ibid., 116.
11. Research findings on CQ and negotiation presented in Lynn Imai and Michele J. Gelfand, "Culturally Intelligent Negotiators: The Impact of CQ on Intercultural Negotiation Effectiveness," *Academy of Management Best Paper Proceedings* (2007).
12. Gary Ferraro, *The Cultural Dimension of Business* (Upper Saddle River, NJ: Prentice-Hall, 1990), 133.
13. David Thomas and Kerr Inkson, *Cultural Intelligence*, 118.
14. L. Imai and M. J. Gelfand, "Culturally Intelligent Negotiators: The Impact of CQ on Intercultural Negotiation Effectiveness," *Academy of Management Best Paper Proceedings* (2007).
15. Howard Giles and Philip Smith, "Accommodation Theory: Optimal Levels of Convergence" in *Language and Social Psychology*, H. Giles

and R. N. St. Clair, eds. (Baltimore: University Park Press, 1979), 45–63.

Chapter 8   See the Journey Ahead: Proof and Consequences of CQ

1. Thomas Rockstuhl, *Relationships with CQ in Literature* (Singapore: Nanyang Business School, 2008).

2. Soon Ang and Linn Van Dyne, "Conceptualization of Cultural Intelligence" in *Handbook of Cultural Intelligence: Theory, Measurement, and Applications,* Soon Ang and Linn Van Dyne, eds. (Armonk, NY: M.E. Sharpe, 2008), 10.

3. Soon Ang, Linn Van Dyne, C. Koh, K. Y. Ng, K. J. Templer, C. Tay, and N. A. Chandrasekar, "Cultural Intelligence: Its Measurement and Effects on Cultural Judgment and Decision-Making, Cultural Adaptation, and Task Performance," *Management and Organization Review* 3 (2007): 335–371.

4. P. Christopher Earley, Soon Ang, and Joo-Seng Tan, *CQ: Developing Cultural Intelligence at Work* (Stanford, CA: Stanford Business Books, 2006), 10.

5. Economist Intelligence Unit, "CEO Briefing: Corporate Priorities for 2006 and Beyond," in *The Economist: Economic Intelligence Unit* (EIU) at http://a330.g.akamai.net/7/330/25828/20060213195601/graphics.eiu.com/files/ad_pdfs/ceo_Briefing_UKTI_wp.pdf, 14.

6. P. Christopher Earley, Soon Ang, and Joo-Seng Tan, *CQ,* 10.

7. Soon Ang et al., "Cultural Intelligence," 335–371.

8. T. Oolders, O. S. Chernyshenko, and S. Shark, "Cultural Intelligence as a Mediator of Relationships Between Openness to Experience and Adaptive Performance," in *Handbook of Cultural Intelligence: Theory, Measurement, and Applications,* Soon Ang and Linn Van Dyne, eds. (Armonk, NY: M.E. Sharpe, 2008), 145–158; and Soon Ang et al., "Cultural Intelligence."

9. Kwanghyun Kim, Bradley Kirkman, and Gilad Chen, "Cultural Intelligence and International Assignment Effectiveness: A Conceptual Model and Preliminary Findings" in *Handbook of Cultural Intelligence: Theory, Measurement, and Applications,* Soon Ang and Linn Van Dyne, eds. (Armonk, NY: M.E. Sharpe, 2008), 71ff.

10. Economist Intelligence Unit, "CEO Briefing," 14.

11. R. Imai, "The Culturally Intelligent Negotiator: The Impact of CQ on Intercultural Negotiation Effectiveness," *Masters Abstracts International* 45 (2007): 5.

12. P. Christopher Earley, Soon Ang, and Joo-Seng Tan, *CQ*, 10.

13. Soon Ang and Andrew C. Inkpen, "Cultural Intelligence and Offshore Outsourcing Success: A Framework of Firm-Level Intercultural Capability," *Decision Sciences* 39 (August 2008): 346.

14. Cheryl Tay, Mina Westman, and Audrey Chia, "Antecedents and Consequences of Cultural Intelligence Among Short-Term Business Travelers" in *Handbook of Cultural Intelligence: Theory, Measurement, and Applications*, Soon Ang and Linn Van Dyne, eds. (Armonk, NY: M.E. Sharpe, 2008), 126ff.

15. M. V. Lugo, "An Examination of Cultural and Emotional Intelligences in the Development of Global Transformational Leadership Skills," *Dissertation Abstracts International* 68 (2007): 10; and K. A. Crowne, "The Relationship Among Social Intelligence, Emotional Intelligence, Cultural Intelligence, and Cultural Exposure," *Dissertation Abstracts International* 68 (2007): 3.

16. Soon Ang, Linn Van Dyne, and Christine Koh, "Personality Correlates of the Four-Factor Model of Cultural Intelligence," *Group & Organizational Management* 31 (2006): 100–123.

17. Efrat Shokef and Miriam Erea, "Cultural Intelligence and Global Identity in Multicultural Teams" in *Handbook of Cultural Intelligence: Theory, Measurement, and Applications*, Soon Ang and Linn Van Dyne, eds. (Armonk, NY: M.E. Sharpe, 2008), 180.

18. Cheryl Tay, Mina Westman, and Audrey Chia, "Antecedents and Consequences of Cultural Intelligence Among Short-Term Business Travelers," 126–144; Soon Ang et al., "Cultural Intelligence"; and L. M. Shannon and T. M. Begley, "Antecedents of the Four-Factor Model of Cultural Intelligence" in *Handbook of Cultural Intelligence: Theory, Measurement, and Applications*, Soon Ang and Linn Van Dyne, eds. (Armonk, NY: M.E. Sharpe, 2008), 41–55.

19. Cheryl Tay, Mina Westman, and Audrey Chia, "Antecedents and Consequences," 126–144.

20. Efrat Shokef and Miriam Erea, "Cultural Intelligence and Global Identity in Multicultural Teams," 177–191.

21. Kok Yee Ng, Linn Van Dyne, and Soon Ang, "From Experience to Experiential Learning: Cultural Intelligence as a Learning Capability for Global Leader Development," *Academy of*

Management Learning & Education (forthcoming).

22. See Ranya Idliby, Suzanne Oliver, and Priscilla Warner, *The Faith Club: A Muslim, A Christian, A Jew — Three Women Search for Understanding* (New York: Free Press, 2006) for a true-life account of three women who did just this.

Chapter 9 Recruit Travel Companions: Developing CQ in Your Team

1. Edgar Schein, *Organizational Culture and Leadership* (San Francisco: Jossey-Bass, 2004), 23.
2. Soon Ang and Andrew C. Inkpen, "Cultural Intelligence and Offshore Outsourcing Success: A Framework of Firm-Level Intercultural Capability," *Decision Sciences* 39 (August 2008): 343–344; and M. A. Carpenter, W. G. Sanders, and H. B. Gregersen, "Bundling Human Capital with Organizational Context: The Impact of International Assignment Experience on Multinational Firm Performance and CEO Pay," *Academy Management Journal* 44 (2001): 493–511.
3. Margaret Shaffer and Gloria Miller, "Cultural Intelligence: A Key Success Factor for Expatriates," in *Handbook of Cultural Intelligence: Theory, Measurement, and Applications*, Soon Ang and Linn Van Dyne, eds. (Armonk, NY: M.E. Sharpe, 2008), 107ff.
4. Cheryl Tay, Mina Westman, and Audrey Chia, "Antecedents and Consequences of Cultural Intelligence Among Short-Term Business Travelers" in *Handbook of Cultural Intelligence: Theory, Measurement, and Applications*, Soon Ang and Linn Van Dyne, eds. (Armonk, NY: M.E. Sharpe, 2008), 130.
5. Soon Ang and Andrew C. Inkpen, "Cultural Intelligence and Offshore Outsourcing Success," 346.
6. Jiing-Lih Larry Farh, P. Christopher Earley, and Shu-Chi Lin, "Impetus for Action: A Cultural Analysis of Justice and Organizational Citizenship Behavior in Chinese Society," *Administrative Science Quarterly* 42 (1997): 421–444.
7. Rebecca Kuiper, personal conversation (October 2, 2008).
8. Maddy Janssens and Tineke Cappellen, "Contextualizing Cultural Intelligence: The Case of Global Managers," in *Handbook of Cultural Intelligence: Theory, Measurement, and Applications*, Soon Ang and Linn Van Dyne, eds. (Armonk, NY: M.E. Sharpe, 2008), 369.

9. P. Christopher Earley, Soon Ang, and Joo-Seng Tan, *CQ: Developing Cultural Intelligence at Work* (Stanford, CA: Stanford Business Books, 2006), 29.

10. Michael Goh, Julie M. Koch, and Sandra Sanger, "Cultural Intelligence in Counseling Psychology," in *Handbook of Cultural Intelligence: Theory, Measurement, and Applications*, Soon Ang and Linn Van Dyne, eds. (Armonk, NY: M.E. Sharpe, 2008), 264.

11. Fareed Zakaria, *The Post-American World* (New York: Norton Publishing 2008), 225.

Appendix: Research Context

1. R. Sternberg and D. K. Detterman, *What Is Intelligence? Contemporary Viewpoints on Its Nature and Definition* (New York: Ablex Publishing, 1986).

2. Soon Ang, Linn Van Dyne, C. Koh, K. Y. Ng, K. J. Templer, C. Tay, and N. A. Chandrasekar, "Cultural Intelligence: Its Measurement and Effects on Cultural Judgment and Decision-Making, Cultural Adaptation, and Task Performance," *Management and Organization Review* 3 (2007): 335–371.

3. Soon Ang and Linn Van Dyne, eds., *Handbook of Cultural Intelligence: Theory, Measurement, and Applications* (Armonk, NY: M.E. Sharpe, 2008), 130. This volume offers the most extensive publication of CQ research to date.

culture
  core values, 90–106
  high vs. low context, 96
  impact on behavior, 69
  values, by regions and nations,
    90
  viewing role of, 67–74
culture intent, 190
customers, understanding, 15

decision making, 165–166
  systems, 190–191
delivery of message, 145–146
distance, and communication, 147
diversity training, 36
  approach to, 26
  failure, 42–43
divisional training, for learning CQ,
  192
Dyne, Linn Van, 30, 199

Earley, Christopher, xiv, 199
Eastern cultures, 85–86
eating, 49–53, 173
economic systems, 75–76
Economist's CEO Briefing, 15
education, 24
  formal systems vs. informal, 79,
    80
education level, 171
emerging markets, demand from,
  15
emotional intelligence (EQ), vs.
  cultural intelligence, 32–34
emotional stability, 170
employer of choice, 167–168
environmental responsibility, 56
ethnocentrism, 64, 109–110
event time
  and apology for lateness, 142
  vs. clock time, 92–93, 94
expansion, international, 167

expatriates, assignment termina-
  tion, 17
experiences, 172–173
extroversion, 170
extrinsic motivation, 26
eye contact, 149

facial expression, 148–149
faith club, 174
family systems, 76–78
fear of losing face, 97
feedback, 158
films, 172–173
Finland, power distance level, 101
flat world, 5
  and business operations, 12
flexibility, 166
  in negotiation, 152
Flint, Doug, 167
fluid artistic systems, 85–87
food, 49–53, 173
  strategies for trying new, 51
formal education systems, vs.
  informal, 79, 80
France, 102
  cultural values, 91
  phrasing requests in, 141–142
Friedman, Thomas, 5

Germany, 102–104
  conversation topics, 139
  participative leadership style, 18
  power distance level, 101
  Wal-Mart failure, 65
gestures, 148
Ghana, formal respect to leaders,
  100
global identity, 171
global networks, 54–55
globalization, 5
Greece, 102
grocery store, 175

Index

David Livermore, Ph.D. (Michigan State University), is the executive director of the Global Learning Center in Grand Rapids, Michigan. In addition, David is a visiting research fellow at Nanyang Technological University in Singapore and a senior research consultant with the Cultural Intelligence Center in East Lansing, Michigan. Dave has done training and consulting with leaders in seventy-five countries across the Americas, Africa, Asia, Australia, and Europe. (Visit his website at www.davidlivermore. com.)